*Nor Iron Bars a Cage*

# Nor Iron Bars a Cage

## PENELOPE TREMAYNE

HEINEMANN : LONDON

William Heinemann Ltd
10 Upper Grosvenor Street, London W1X 9PA

LONDON   MELBOURNE
JOHANNESBURG   AUCKLAND

First published 1988
Copyright © Penelope Tremayne 1988

British Library Cataloguing in Publication Data

Tremayne, Penelope
    Nor iron bars a cage.
    1. Sri Lanka — History — 1948—
    2. Hostages — Sri Lanka
    3. British — Sri Lanka
    I. Title
    954'9'303'0924          DS489.84
    ISBN 0 434 79116 4

Printed in Great Britain by
Richard Clay Ltd, Bungay, Suffolk

Stone walls do not a prison make
Nor iron bars a cage.


Richard Lovelace
'To Althea, From Prison'

THE hills above Kandy in Sri Lanka must be among the most nearly perfect in the world: a country as blue and precipitous and exquisite as those we imagine in childhood, full of forests and waterfalls and spice-gardens, sparkling with butterflies and birds. Tony and I went there in May of 1985.

The beauty of those mountains is like a drug. To look into them at sunset was like looking across the Parnon range in the Peloponnese; they are bigger but have the same general pattern and outlines, the same shades of soft and intense and darkening blue, the same recessions, one shoulder behind another and another. There were moments when you could count eight, nine, ten at a time. Such views — and they are rare — can take possession of you, for as your imagination climbs each crest away into infinity you know that something unique is to be seen behind each. A line of hills across your view calls you to only one climb, but hills enfiladed to you signal that if you take one you must take them all.

Yet there were signs that the serpent was in Eden. Guards with side-arms stood at the gates of the spice-gardens. To guard whom? Against what? No, we were told, this was not Tamil-held territory. But a lot of the pickers were Tamils; more than once men had come up here covertly trying to stir them up to acts of violence. We knew that for some years trouble had been brewing between Tamils and Sinhalese in the island; that there had been bomb incidents, and tourists were therefore thin on the ground. But we knew neither the origins nor the rights and wrongs of it, and did not want to learn them.

We had come here for peace and quiet, not to be drawn

1

into a quarrel that did not concern us. The sunsets were cosmic carnivals, and each night as they faded lightning-storms replaced them, great thunderheads of cloud flashing messages back and forth like titanic heliographs to each other across half the sky. These displays after dark were so glorious that it was hard to leave them and go indoors to eat or sleep.

In May the monsoon reaches the great, dreamy beaches of the south and west and wraps them in rain. I could have stayed for ever up here in the hills, among the towering trees and clouds and cascades and little shining clove-bushes. But we went down at last, north-eastwards through steep forests and idyllic valleys full of egrets and paddy-birds and the brilliant green of young rice; then low jungle and the sandy plain that lies behind Trincomalee. We went to a hotel near the village of Nilaveli, a few miles north of the great desolate harbour, and this place too seemed like a paradise of a different kind. There was a garden with meticulously swept gravel paths half-lost in a foam of flowering shrubs and creepers, and these ran straight down to a white sand beach stretching away in a shallow curve as far as eye could see in either direction. Our bedroom windows looked out over the cockled red-tile roof of a long veranda below; every now and then with a crash like a crate of bottles being dropped one of a troop of grey langurs would leap down on to it from the trees, smashing tiles all round him. The rooftop was littered with sherds like an archaeologist's fantasy.

The hotel had rooms for 150 guests. But now there were only eleven, counting ourselves, although prices had been cut ludicrously low in an effort to hold on to what little tourist trade could survive. Alongside us was a similar hotel, in similar straits. The beach was common to both but no one felt crowded.

The swimming was superb, though with a strong northerly current running at about two knots, parallel with the shore. We liked walking south along the beach before breakfast, while the horizon was still milky and the sun benign, then flopping

2

into the water and letting the current double our swimming speed on the way back. There would be one or two fishermen about at this time, and children going along the beach to school in a village nearby. And sometimes women going down to the next village to sell embroideries would try to interest us, calling to us from the shallows. They had smiles like angels and would wade in up to their knees, holding out scarves or tablecloths, looking like wet butterflies in their bright saris and seeming to imagine that we carried money in our swimsuits or could catch it out of the gleaming surf.

But there were other passers-by, too: young men who would saunter out from the trees and accost us in English, asking where we came from, how long we intended to stay, where else in the island we had been or planned to go. They were polite but subtly arrogant, with a manner we had come to know in other 'troubled' places. We asked our hotel manager about them. Yes, he said, their presence was disquieting. They had been moving in over the last few weeks, walking through the village as if they owned it, levying contributions in cash to their 'cause', letting it be seen that they had arms. They lived somewhere in the jungle, but came and went as they chose. Yes, they were Tamils, but not local. No one here or in the village had seen them before or knew where they came from.

Tony and I did not mean to give up our peace and quiet. We had read only what the English Press had reported about the problem: that the Tamils were an innocent, impoverished, harmless minority and that the Sinhalese, including the army and the police, Nazi-like uniformed thugs, regularly hunted them through the woods like vermin and killed them. We had seen no sign of this, but that was no proof that it did not happen. Nor were Press stories any proof that it did.

The shadows were lengthening faster than we knew. Access to the hotel was by the one road which runs up the east coast of the island. One morning a land-mine was detonated under an army truck, blowing a twelve-foot-wide crater and leaving two men dead and seven wounded. The man who had sat under a tree a few yards away and set it off, and the man who had signalled the truck's approach from a corner, both got safely away. The road being now impassable, the wounded were carried through the garden of the hotel next to ours and put into its boat for transport to hospital in Trincomalee. That night seventeen armed men, some with stockings over their faces, attacked that hotel, lined up the staff at gunpoint, and stripped out the safe. Departing, they said this was a 'punishment', because the manager had allowed the wounded through. Two of the leaders of these avenging angels had seemed to be foreigners: that is, they had talked to each other in a language which neither the Tamil nor the Sinhalese staff could understand.

All at once it had become impossible to keep closed eyes.

Next morning our hotel manager was absent, and the staff — mostly Tamils with a few Sinhalese — carried on, smiling uneasily and with punctilious attention to detail. Five of the other guests departed, leaving only a diplomatic couple on leave and a pair of honeymooners who would probably not have noticed if a nuclear device had been exploded.

The manager (a Sinhalese) returned the next day; he had taken his wife and child down to safety in Colombo and left them there. He brought us our passports and travellers' cheques out of the hotel safe, where we had been advised on arrival to keep them — largely because a grey langur would sometimes get into a room. Now he asked us to take charge of them ourselves. What had happened next door was bound to happen here, he said, before long.

We had hoped to stay another week, but it seemed only fair to ask him whether he would prefer all guests to leave, so that he could close the hotel. He said no. He had talked it over with the staff, and they had all agreed to stick it out as long as they could. 'But,' he said, 'I have had to tell them that we shall all be without jobs in a week or two: say a month at most.'

We stayed on, not quite so green and detached as we had

4

been before, for our week. We planned to spend our last two nights in the Wilpattu game reserve. This is one of the last places where wild leopard may still be seen, and what is more, seen in daylight. On the way there we should spend a night at Anuradhapura, the ancient royal capital. The most revered Buddhist shrine in the island is there, under the outspread arms of a gigantic peepul tree, said to be a cutting from a sapling of a northern Indian tree under which the Buddha himself once sat. It may well be the oldest living tree in the world.

On our last morning at Nilaveli forty armed Tamils, dressed in camouflage kit like that worn by the Sri Lankan Army, hijacked two buses, shot the drivers, and drove themselves into Anuradhapura. Here they opened fire on the normal morning crowd of worshippers and gossipers in front of the Bo Tree temple, and in the ensuing panic drove away again leaving 149 dead, men, women, and children, and many more injured.

All roads in and out of Anuradhapura were closed, but it was a case of the horse and the stable-door. The security forces still relied for communications on the totally inefficient civilian telephone system. It was several hours before details of what had been done had reached Colombo and orders had gone back out to appropriate units. One vehicle-load of police had tried to give chase on their own initiative; but, impeded by logs across the road at the entrances to villages (put there by themselves in the hope of impeding terrorists), they soon realized they had lost the trail. So, not knowing what to do, they sat down and had tea. The murderers meanwhile had made off for Wilpattu Game Park. This place, like all its kind, is kept going by earnings from tourism, and had been faring this year as badly as the hotels. When the game wardens saw two buses swing in through the gate they thought their luck had turned, and they and their families came out to make the visitors welcome. When they saw their mistake it was too late. The gang shot them down, all but one who, having been out all night, had stayed in bed and so was missed.

An army helicopter sighted the buses and even saw some of the terrorists heading off into the jungle. The helicopter was not mounted with machine-guns, but one of the crew managed to throw out a couple of hand-grenades and, it was thought, killed four. The rest made their way, in their own time, down to beaches on the west coast whence they were picked up in boats (no doubt by prearrangement) and carried to safety.

We would have stayed on to learn more, but we were under the modern traveller's most depressing and inescapable compulsion, the need to catch a given flight on a given day. Three days later we reached London, and the next morning learned from an inch of print in *The Times* that our hotel at Nilaveli had been totally demolished. A statement put out by a Tamil group was quoted, saying that they had destroyed the hotel because the army were about to use the place as a base from which to harry the freedom-fighters.

Knowing this to be untrue I rang the appropriate editorial desk and offered some accurate background. But no one was interested. When Sunday came, one of the main newspapers carried a harrowing half-page article by a correspondent who had managed to make contact with the Tamil rebels (he did not say, perhaps did not know, that they normally hung about the main hotels on the look-out for journalists in search of a story). They had taken him to what they said was the scene of a crime committed ten days before by the security forces, and told him a horrifying tale which he passed on whole to his readers. It referred to an incident which had taken place while we were still in the island. I had followed accounts of it from different sources, and it was fairly clear that what had really happened was not much like the version now in print. So I sent in an alternative account. The Foreign Features Editor said that it was too long, but that if I cut it to 400 words he would print it. Two hours later it was back on his desk in 392 words, partly as follows:

. . . On May 17th the security forces reported that, acting on a tip-off from locals, they had attacked a terrorist training-camp south of Batticaloa. At least 75 men escaped; still the SF claimed 18 killed and assorted equipment seized: explosives, shoes, 23 bicycles, 20 photographs of trainees, etc. Twenty more terrorists were captured later, including two wanted members of PLOTE (People's Liberation Organization of Tamil Eelam) and two members of EPRLF (Eelam People's Revolutionary Liberation Front). They assessed that about 200 terrorists had been in the area all told.

Later an enterprising western journalist went there, contacted the terrorists, and was told that police had seized some 40 youths suspected of belonging to LTTE (Liberation Tigers of Tamil Eelam), forced them to dig communal graves, shot them, and poured acid on their faces to hinder identification. He saw fragments of rotting human flesh and hair; his escorts said the SF had later redug up the bodies and removed them. But luckily two units of 'Tamil Tigers' (precise group unspecified) with rocket-launchers and cameras, were nearby. They photographed the graves, dug up the bodies and photographed them before the acid had had time to work, and reburied them. They said the pictures were for 'our comrades in India', for publicity use.

It is not for me to say which story, if either, is correct. But: where did the acid come from? Why were the rocket-launchers not used and the captives rescued? And so on. Only the terrorists' version has appeared in our national Press. With the utmost respect, I wonder whether we are not in danger of allowing persistent propaganda to lead us into condoning a terrorism mounted for political ends?

This piece never saw daylight. But meantime another emotive piece had appeared in a national daily, by a journalist who had boarded a local bus going northwards up the island's

7

main road. The other passengers had drawn his attention, out of the bus window, to a grisly charred corpse dangling from a post near the roadside. 'Tamil,' they had said, 'he Tamil.' The journalist had understandably been shaken, and concluded, because the victim was Tamil, that he had been murdered in this horrible way by Sinhalese. He did not know that this was the way in which the Tamil terrorists 'punish' those Tamils whom they identify as trying to make a stand against them, setting up 'executions', and leaving the remains where all can see them, for a warning to others. And so he had reported it as an authentic Sinhalese atrocity.

It is very difficult to see gross misapprehensions taking root and not to speak up; but I knew little more about Sri Lanka than any tourist, and tourists are not normally given credit for being able to tell a goat from a gondola. I began to understand that I should have to go back and learn more. I did so in September 1985, and learned a lot. I saw that Tamil Nationalism had no foundation in real Tamil feelings, but had been invented by Marxist agitators for their own ends; and that the Sri Lankan government, though not tyrannous or oppressive of the minority, had not a notion how to present its case or how to handle the foreign Press.

For some years I had been studying the substitutes for war which have spread round the world, discolouring our times, since 1945: revolutions, terrorist organizations, what Marxist jargon calls 'armed propagandas', and the like; their techniques and their causes. I had been a fairly regular writer on these subjects, for specialist publications. So now I wrote a report describing them in Sri Lanka.

The report found its way to the Foreign Office but they dismissed it as nonsense. They had already decided in their god-like way (I learned later) that the Tamil insurgency was a genuine national movement, and not Marxist at all — or at least they would not accept it as such. In January 1986, how-

8

ever, I was asked to give a talk on the subject in London. The Sri Lankan government gave me a return air ticket so that I could return there to update myself; there were no stipulations about whom I should speak to, where I should go, or what I should say afterwards.

I spent a few days in Colombo, collecting and checking facts. But that was only part of what I had come for. I needed to know what the idea of Tamil Eelam — a separate Tamil state — meant to the people who would live in it if it came about: the small cultivators and shopkeepers and labourers and clerks who had a nationality now, and were said to be in desperate need of another. They were not doing the fighting, but that might mean nothing. Such people rarely can: they are keeping the children fed and the fields watered. But there are ways in which they can show whether the freedom-fighters' goals are their goals too, or so much moonshine to them. And that was what I had come to the island to see.

A regulation was in force, forbidding foreigners from travelling outside the areas where police or armed forces could reasonably protect them. I therefore went to a very senior military commander, and asked him for permission to drive to Mullaitivu, a small fishing town on the north-east coast, deep in the part of the island held by the terrorists. He said that I could try, if I really wanted to. (We both knew the terms on which I had accepted that air ticket: that I should go where I chose.) 'But you will meet the terrorists,' he said. 'Most certainly you will meet them.'

I already knew that the terrorists often patrolled the roads they held (I had met them once before, during that October visit) in the hope of finding some journalist whom they could escort to a house or a camp, where they would fill him up with tales which would make good copy, presenting themselves as both victims and heroes. But I did not want the artificiality of such a conducted tour. If the people of these two provinces wanted independence, well and good; but they could show it best without armed men standing over them.

The General wrote me a *laissez-passer* instructing any military patrol not to turn me back. 'But,' he said, 'the risk is high, and in all fairness I must tell you that if you fall into the terrorists' hands there is practically nothing that we can do to help you.' I asked for a sheet of paper and wrote a letter, saying that the Sri Lankan government was not responsible for me and was under no circumstances to enter into any bargains on my behalf with 'undesirable people'. I was rather proud of this phrase, thought of on the spur of the moment, because it had struck me that if I specified 'Tamils' or 'terrorists' or 'guerrillas' or anything else the people involved could persuade the Sri Lankan authorities that they did not match the definition, and pressure to bargain could after all be applied.

I must make it clear that the General had not asked nor hinted that I should write such a letter, and that he accepted it only with reluctance. I wrote it because I had often considered the problem of whether hostages' lives should be bargained for or not, and knew that whatever the personal feelings involved the right answer is No.

I said goodbye to the General and he wished me luck; I then hired a self-drive Fiat car and drove to the government rest-house at Anuradhapura.

At seven the next morning my friend Nirmala came down to see me off. She is a young woman of exceptional common sense, resourcefulness and charm. She asked me when I aimed to be back in Anuradhapura, and I said, between seven and eight that night. 'Let's think of the worst case,' she said. 'Had I better have Tony's telephone number, in case you're not?' I gave it to her, but urged that she wait twenty-four hours before raising any alarm.

The first thirty-five miles northwards, to Vavuniya, were through friendly – that is, government-held – territory. There was nothing to worry about except the size and suddenness of the pot-holes. Nearly all Sri Lankan roads are kept at a level of disrepair which is hard to credit until you are used to it. Then at Vavuniya there was a long delay caused first by a stationary line of armoured vehicles, then a traffic queue, then a checkpoint at the exit from the town. The cause of it all was a search of the ditch along one side of the road by troops with rifles and mine-detectors. I would have liked to know more about this, but time was not on my side. I had reckoned it would take three to three and a half hours to drive to Mullaitivu, and I wanted a full half-day there. So I was the more annoyed, a bit further on, to come up out of a pot-hole with the sound of rushing air as a tyre went flat.

The wheel-nuts had not been touched for months and nothing I did would shift them. I danced about on the end of the wheel-brace as usefully as a toad on a harrow, but gradually realized that there was nothing to be done until the next vehicle came along. This was not real Injun-country, only half-and-half; that is, the government held the road, and the terrorists held the hinterland and used the road when they thought they could risk it. My main worry was that the army convoy would catch up with me. They would change the wheel for me, and the General's letter would ensure that they let me go on; but they might take a very long time about it.

After ten minutes a battered civilian lorry hove in sight. The driver slowed down to take a careful look as he passed, then pulled in to the verge and came back to offer help. A very dark, very lightly built young Tamil, he could no more shift the nuts than I; nor could his older, heavier mate, who had a little English and a heavy spanner with which he belaboured the brace. A second lorry pulled up, more tools were brought, and at last the job was done. They had all been keeping a weather eye out as they worked. I offered them money for their pains, but they refused it with smiles and gentle mumbles. The English-speaker asked me where I was going. I said 'Mullaitivu', knowing that it was stupid of me to be, as it were, blazing a trail in front of myself, but not caring.

11

It would have been uncourteous to lie to those who had helped me, but there was more to it than that: this trip was developing a quality of its own. There is a special flavour to such conversations with strangers, when they may be lethal to you, or you to them, and neither you nor they know which way up the coin lies.

They all looked very dubious, and the English-speaker said, 'Will they let you go?' 'Who?' I asked, wondering what he would say. He said, 'The army.' I laughed and said, 'If not, I shall have to come back.' I could see that he wanted to ask more, but had not enough English, might not even have understood what I had said so far. He spoke briefly with the other three and then said that I must stop and get the punctured tyre mended in Mankulam, five miles on. He would go ahead of me and lead me there. He was right: it would have been insane to travel those roads without a spare. I asked him if Mankulam would have petrol and he said yes, maybe.

Fiats have small tanks; a fill-up at Vavuniya had given me enough to get back there after Mullaitivu, but not much more. I was now going to be running an hour and a half to two hours behind schedule, including time to have the puncture mended. By the time I got back to Vavuniya the filling-station would be shut, so I must get another fill-up elsewhere. But as a means of limiting the terrorists' movements the government had closed petrol stations except in the main towns where they could be guarded; otherwise the terrorists seized the petrol for their own use, and sold what they did not need at black-market prices. So it was important for me to buy petrol where I could.

At Mankulam a surly-looking man said he had no petrol, but there would be some in Mullaitivu. He gave my tyre to a boy to patch, and went away — which was not normal behaviour. A long time passed. I thought that if he was working for the terrorists he would tell the boy to work slowly, and meanwhile send someone to fetch them. But no; it was a big patch and had to be given time to dry properly, that was all. I

12

had the right change to pay for it, but seeing a larger note in my handbag he picked it out and said he would break it up into small ones for me. If I needed money further on, he said, I might not find people willing to do this. If true it seemed to imply an uneasy economy. The wheel was put back on the car at last — the spare had looked hardly fit to bear the weight of a bicycle — and I drove off.

The atmosphere of Mankulam was not good. Vavuniya had been like some small frontier town liable to sudden raids: the people are law-abiding and anxious to please, but tense, aware that more than that may be needed from them at any moment. Mankulam was only a straggly village strung out along the road. It ought to have been swarming with children, people, dogs, cows, carts; rippling with light-tongued chatter. But there was no one about at all and half the houses were shuttered — some no doubt because they were empty, their owners fled; others, by the feel of it, with scared women lying low behind fastened doors. I realized that the garage owner had kept away from me not because he lacked curiosity but because my presence was a potential danger.

From Mankulam to Mullaitivu is about thirty miles of narrow white dust road — an hour to an hour and a half's driving time, depending on the state of the road surface, of culverts, and so on. There was cultivation on both sides at first: good farming land, well kept up. Then there was jungle. I had heard that there were wild elephant here, and hoped to see one, but my luck was out. The verges of the road were cleared back for ten or fifteen yards on either side, leaving only an occasional tree or two to make a pool of shade for passers-by. In one of them I stopped to eat the picnic lunch I had brought from Anuradhapura.

The lush spring grass looked fragile and tender, a pale silvery green scattered thinly with flowers. But minute by minute the feeling grew on me that I was being watched.

13

Later and in the light of events I thought that I had been wrong about this: it had been no more than the shadow of things to come. But, true or false, it spoiled what could and should have been fifteen minutes of perfect ease.

In spite of this disquiet, I was conscious of a deep tranquillity that filled the afternoon. There was a fragile natural silence here, and the trees, of many different kinds and heights, had a lightness of foliage which gave them extraordinary grace. The morning had been sultry, but now broad sweeps of the sky had cleared. As I drove on again it showed a tender Tibetan-poppy blue with none of the crude brilliance that can afflict the tropics. The blue was broken by a few big, pillowy clouds, thistledown-white just faintly tinged with pink and gold by shafts of sun striking on one cloud from behind another, although the afternoon was still young.

By now I knew that I was probably driving to my death. (I have been asked why, once I had drawn that conclusion, I did not turn round and drive back the way I had come. I can find no answer that stands up in logic or common sense. I suppose that the reason for all our follies — as well as any strokes we may possibly bring off right — lies in our human nature.) The thought oppressed me much less than its equal and opposite fear, that my luck might hold too well and I might pass right through the terrorists' country and out again without having encountered them at all. Then I should lose at least half of what I had come to learn. I should have wasted other people's effort and perhaps have been a fool, to very little purpose. An exceptional opportunity would have been lost.

I can see now that I was not thinking logically. Of course, if I did not run across the terrorists, I could not learn anything about them, but if I did meet them it was likely that I should not live to make use of the lesson.

I began to want very much to know whether I could look at death without shrinking — not just during the moment between when the shot is about to be fired and the discovery that it has or has not hit you, but during slow hours of waiting

14

to be killed; for then the temptation to buy your freedom by saying what your captors want must be great. But again, what use would this knowledge be to me if I did not survive the getting it?

I meant to think out this and other problems sensibly, as I went; but instead my mind filled with thoughts that I had not been prepared for. I was carried away by the beauty of the afternoon and the place, by their pristine glory and innocence and by a growing consciousness of the extraordinary kindness of God in letting me enjoy such beauty for my last hours of life. That they should be the last wakened not the least regret: on the contrary, I saw that it would be wrong and churlish, having been shown so perfectly how good the world is, to ask for more of it. I had had all I deserved and much more.

While these thoughts held me, the car-driving part of my mind made me slow down with the notion that something nearby was on fire; it had seemed for an instant that clouds of white ash, such as a bonfire of papers produces, were blowing across the road. The next moment I saw that it was not white ash but white butterflies, thousands upon thousands of them, dancing in the space between the jungle and the road, filling the air from about four feet above ground up to about twenty feet. I drove forward at a walking pace, and they fluttered upwards clear of the car roof or sideways into the slipstream. I must have been moving through them for a hundred yards or more; and a mile further on I came into another long cloud of them, I think many more still. It struck me that I was seeing one of the real marvels of nature — probably a seasonal one but that did not make it any the less astonishing. I felt more privileged and lucky than ever, and began to put a poem together as I went along. It did not get finished at that time, because the concentration needed for writing poetry is not compatible with car-driving, and I always have to thrust it down rather than end up in a ditch.

The jungle gave way to tended fields once more, then on the skyline — not very far away in that dead-flat country —

15

palm-tree tops appeared, and angles of roofs gleaming between them. I reached a fork in the road: ahead it ran straight for perhaps half a mile and vanished in a clump of trees. A smaller, rougher road led off to the right, and also was lost in trees; but behind these trees I could see signs of houses again. I had a map and had read it carefully, but it was not detailed enough to show this junction. I was keeping straight ahead when I saw in the mirror that a man with a bicycle had appeared at the fork and was looking very hard at me. There seemed to be not much point in asking for directions: if the road I was on did bypass the town there would certainly be another road coming out from the town to meet it. But instinct spoke loudly to me, and I backed up towards the man with the bicycle and said 'Mullaitivu?'

He nodded.

'Which way?'

'Both.' He had not much English, but just enough. He indicated the road straight ahead and said: 'Army camp.' I had not been told that there was one here, but I knew enough to realize that it must be maintained under siege conditions, as the camps in Jaffna were, supplied by air or by armed convoy at longish intervals, and sending out no patrols. None the less its officer would probably be willing to let me have three gallons of petrol, and it would be as well for him to know where I was in case of trouble later. I thanked the man with the bicycle and began to slide forward again. He looked at me hard and oddly for a moment, then stepped to one side, making the smallest of movements with one hand towards the right fork. 'Better go this way,' he murmured. And so compelling was his barely audible, hesitant voice that I put the wheel over and did as he suggested. When I had almost reached the first trees and houses I looked in the mirror. He was still standing there. I shall never know why he spoke as he did. Perhaps there was a land-mine on the other road; perhaps he had laid it himself (why else was he there?). Much later in the afternoon I heard a heavy crump. But by then I had other things to worry about.

More likely he knew what company I should meet in the town, and knew that if I had been to the army camp they would kill me for it.

I drove along tree-lined roads, very quiet, and came rather suddenly into what I could see was the main street of Mullaitivu. It was dirty and unkempt but busy with cars and bicycles; I was a potential obstruction when I stopped to look for a petrol sign. One or two people stared or hooted, then a bicyclist dismounted and in excellent English asked if he could help me. I said I was looking for a petrol station.

'There is one,' he said. 'But they have no petrol.'

Was there any to be had from anywhere? 'The army would let you have some,' he said, 'if you went to the camp.'

'Which way is the camp, please?' But he hummed and hawed and it became clear that he did not mean me to go there. At last he said that if I went to the Catholic church I could probably get some. The priest could often arrange it.

I knew from of old that there is no better source of reliable information about how a community is living and where its heart is than a beleaguered Catholic priest. 'Follow my bicycle,' the man said. 'I will lead you.' And we set off through the streets, with stares and shouted questions following us.

The church of St Peter stood almost on the sea-shore, divided from it only by the stone wall of a biggish open compound. The main door of the church gave on to a road running down to the beach; at the back another door opened into the compound, where were the mission house and a big church room with barn-like doors facing seaward. The bicyclist told me to leave the car in the compound, and led me into the church room. He explained that he was working voluntarily in Mullaitivu, part-time, among the refugees; and went to fetch the priest.

Father Albert was a tall, skeletally thin young Tamil with the bright, sunken eyes of total faith and overwork nearing

17

exhaustion. His parish ran from Jaffna to Trincomalee: more than 120 miles, and the few roads mostly closed or impassable. His real preoccupation was with the Tamil refugees. Most were from Colombo or Trincomalee. Some had fled to escape real danger, some because Tamil politicians had told them to, some simply because others had gone and they had become infected with collective fear. The most tragic were the small children who in the stampede had been separated from their parents and families, and did not know who they were or where they came from. Father Albert had been looking after as many as forty-five not long before, here in the mission house, with the help of his little sister, Queen Elizabeth, who was his house-keeper. Now government aid was beginning to arrive, and things were better. Only four or five children were still on his hands. But there was a very long way to go, still, and no foreseeing when there would be an end to it.

Listening to these two men I began to understand the plight of the ordinary Tamil, loyal to his own people and caught between the millstones. And I began wondering what overseas help might be brought here. Red Cross? Save the Children Fund? They would need reliable figures. The refugee worker opened his briefcase and produced sheets of statistics.

I had temporarily forgotten about politics and terrorism – we were immersed in a practical problem – when a hullabaloo broke out in the compound. Father Albert told me to stay where I was, and went to look.

Outside were half a dozen armed men, with fifteen or twenty more unarmed men and boys milling round them. They had opened the doors of my car and were rootling inside it like dogs at a garbage pail. They were not a reassuring-looking lot. Swaggering and autocratic, they also gave off a strong impression of being both ruthless and hysterical: a combination that boded no good. But by far the worst thing about them was the tone in which they spoke to the few outsiders there –

18

fishermen or other passers-by who, like people anywhere hearing a row in progress, had come to see what was afoot. The self-appointed freedom-fighters spoke to them as if they were rats or less. I had never heard a human voice loaded with such arrogance and contempt, even for some noxious or disgusting animal, and I thought, this is what 'liberation' has come to mean. It lit a red rage in me and I hardly noticed that they were now pouring into the room. Then one of the most arrogant-eyed of them was speaking to me, saying, 'Give your keys.' Glaring back I said, 'What for? The car's open.'

'You are not leaving here,' he replied and made a movement to grab my bag, but someone got in the way quickly. Father Albert was beside me now. He said, 'For your own sake, give them.' He spoke quietly but his eyes were desperate. I said, 'I'll give them to you, Father, but to no one else. The car is not mine.' And I gave them to him. A surge of bodies pushed one way and the other, hands grasping. In moments they had got them from him and were pouring out into the yard again. I supposed they would now steal the car, but a sort of powwow began. The volunteer worker came back in and we both sat down. I tried to go on with the refugee lists, and so did he, but it was difficult. I asked what they were arguing about outside.

'They want to take you away somewhere into the jungle.'
'What for?'
'They say, to ask you some questions.'
'Why don't they ask them here?'
'Father Albert said that. I think they will kill you.'

I did not ask 'What for?' again, because we were clearly not playing a game with rational rules.

The shouting began again; then one of them called angrily for me to come outside, and I went. Father Albert looked as taut as fence-wire but he was unbeaten. One of the bully-boys was sitting in the driving-seat. He spoke furiously at me and Father Albert said he was accusing me of having given him the wrong keys: these did not fit. I saw at once that he simply

19

did not know how to start the car (she was not easy). Father Albert said, 'I have made them say they will not take the car, but they say, nor must you move from here. The car must go there' — he pointed to a sort of recess between the walls of the church and the house — 'and you must not go near it again.' I said, 'Tell him to get out, and I'll put it there.' There was a bit of argument, others now wanting to take the lead, but at last the man in the car moved over, and with everyone watching for sleight-of-hand with another key I drove her in.

They had lost face through this incident, and oddly the fact gave us a breathing space. The priest told me to go back indoors to the refugee worker, and after ten minutes or so he joined us there. Outside, things had become much quieter. They had gone away for a consultation, he said. But they would be back. And most of the hangers-on were still clustered round the gate. Father Albert said there was a guest-room in the church house; I must spend the night there. The volunteer worker agreed.

Neither of these men thought that I should get out alive, and I could see that they were probably right. The important thing therefore, now, was that they should not be killed along with me. I could see quite clearly (this sounds like exaggeration, but such things are not in the least absurd or difficult once the chips are down) that if the terrorists tried to take me by force from his house Father Albert would try to stop them by force, as a man and a Christian. To be those things often brings death, once societies go wrong. I could think of no way to prevent it except by leaving, at once, before the baboon-troop got back. No doubt they would intercept me; but things could then reach a conclusion without involving anyone else. I did not say this to Father Albert, only urging that I wanted to leave, but he insisted that that would add to the danger for everyone, and that I must at least wait until the result of the consultation was known.

By the time they came darkness was falling. Perhaps they had waited for it. They brought a new Comrade with them, a clean-shaven young man of perhaps twenty-two or twenty-three, who had better English than the others. They said that they had come to question me here and now; and they crowded into the priest's small study, about ten of them, with the young inquisitor lounging in an armchair and the others standing or squatting round him. I was given a chair facing them, and the volunteer worker sat at Father Albert's desk, to help with translation if required. Father Albert stayed outside at first, calming down the rabble in the compound, but later he joined us.

I was now — we all were — in the hands of the People's Revolutionary Organization of Tamil Eelam, usually called PLOTE. I expected to be asked why I was here, what I was doing, and so on. But the first question was: 'What do you think of our movement?'

I looked at the boy's face. It was brightly polite, inviting and expecting me to say how much I sympathized with Tamil suffering, or how much I should like to see the freedom-fighters' lairs: anything to convey that I was on their side or convertible to it. But I could see no reason why I should. I thought that this was the last chance I should ever have to hear what these people were like from their own mouths, or to tell them how their ideas and actions looked to others. I said I thought that their movement was a very great mistake.

'Why do you say that?' Faces showed astonishment or anger.

I said that, first, it was not a real movement at all, because the ordinary Tamil people were not behind them. The boy might have said that I could not know that, and I hardly did, as yet, though I did soon enough. But in his turn he could not know how much I already knew. He said, 'Some are frightened now. But they will thank us, when we have won.' I said that they would never thank him except at gunpoint, because he and his movement would strip them of all they had and turn them into slaves.

21

Why did I say that? Well, were he and his friends not Communists? Yes, of course. And most Tamils were not? No, but . . . And a stock diatribe followed.

I said that in any case Eelam could not conceivably be a viable state economically. This was disputed at length. Did I not know how rich was the agricultural land up here? Some of the best in the world. (I thought of all those propaganda statements I had read about the plight of the Tamils penned into waterless semi-desert.) Eelam would not only feed itself, it would export food. The only reason why it was not doing so now was that the government deliberately denied it machinery and modern technology, to keep the output low and the people in slavery. Properly equipped, one man could produce twice what he could now.

Would there not then be an unemployment problem, with no jobs in the south to go to, and the population doubled from the influx of all the Tamils now living and working in the south?

Not at all: great factories were to be built, Eelam would become an industrial power.

Would that not reduce the land and water available for agriculture? And where would the capital come from, to set it all up and keep it going? From the wealthy Tamil communities of Malaysia, Singapore and the USA.

The talk went on like this, Cloud-cuckoo-land floating more clearly into view with each topic raised. If I doubted that the Tamils were exploited, they said, look at education: even official statistics showed that since the present government took power, not one school had been built in the north or east. Luckily I had read the relevant figures, and knew that there are still more schools per head of the population in the north and east than anywhere else in the island. Yes, they said, but that was irrelevant. There was a clear policy to lower Tamil standards. And so on.

Often I saw the voluntary worker signalling to me to go more carefully, and several times when he was translating I think he toned things down. But I was in the grip of an illogical feeling: that since this conversation was going to end in a shooting I had better say everything I could while the chance lasted. There would never be another. (The more reasonable thought, that less intransigence might lead to another, somehow did not present itself.) Probably none of these men was capable of seeing what Tamil Eelam would be like in fact, but I had not yet grasped how low is the mentality of terrorists. I knew that there are few things more futile than to talk in practical terms to Communists: they live in a plastic bubble of myth and fantasy. But I kept thinking: if one grain of reality gets through to even one of them, in retrospect, so that a week or a year hence he wonders, was there something in that, after all? — then it's worth it.

And at last the spokesman got to the core of his ideas. It might even be true, he said, that Tamil Eelam could not support itself; but there was no need for it to do so. Enough money was coming from abroad to get it started; and it had only to keep going for a year or eighteen months.

And then? I asked. Well, that time would not have been wasted in setting up a bourgeois system, it would have been devoted to co-ordination with the Sinhalese comrades in the south and west. As soon as both sides were ready the signal would be given for the People's Revolution to be unleashed; the government and the ruling class would go down — they were already rotten through and through — and the Party would take control of the entire island. I asked if there were enough Sinhalese Communists for this, and he said, yes. They were very well organized, so numbers hardly mattered; the different parties had been working together for a long time, and plans were already well advanced.

And this unitary one-party state would have a Tamil leader? Yes, he said, and licked his lips nervously.

I looked round the priest's study: the bare simplicity and poverty and cleanliness of it, the redolence of hard work and devotion; the cheap desk with its hard chair, the one better

23

chair for visitors in which this callow delinquent lounged, the home-made shelves for papers and the crucifix above the desk. And I thought of all those costly and portentous international conferences where delegates loaded to the gunwales with good intent and self-appreciation would discuss the will of the Tamil people for self-determination. Were these depraved children the Tamil people? I had seen and heard how they treated the Tamil people, outside in the compound. As well suppose that flick-knife wielders and shopping-bag bombers are the representatives of the British people. But the international negotiators had not seen this sort of thing, and never would. They would see only the professional orators, the real revolutionaries, to whom the will of the people means as much as the paper hat in a Christmas cracker. And just for a moment I thought: Suppose I do get out of here, will anyone in the Foreign Office, or anywhere else, want to hear what these posturing self-worshippers are really like?

I said, 'These are only dreams.'

'You must not say such things,' the volunteer worker whispered desperately in the hubbub that followed. I said — and I was speaking mainly now to a boy of about sixteen who looked rather more intelligent than the rest — that Marxist or no, the Sinhalese would not accept Tamil rule. They would fight it out: and how *could* twelve and a half per cent carry the day over seventy-eight per cent?

The spokesman leaned forward. I was forgetting India, he said. Not less than 30,000 armed and trained Comrades — more if necessary — were available to come over and put their blood-brothers into power.

It was hard to believe that this conversation could really be going on. In innumerable thrillers the device is used of the villains expounding their plans to someone whom they have decided to kill, but I had never imagined that such tongue-loosening takes place in real life. I asked if the Indian government had signalled any kind of assent to such an invasion. He smiled, I thought a little uncomfortably. 'They will,' he said.

'You plan to bring 30,000 men from Tamil Nadu to fight for you here?'

'Yes.'

'And when it's over, how will you get them to go away?'

'What do you mean?' He looked nonplussed. I said that when an army has fought and won in a country richer and more comfortable than its own, it is inclined to stay there. He said there was no question of that. 'These people are our friends.' Yes, I said, that was what the Turkish Cypriots had thought about the Turks. It was twelve years now since they had asked them in, and the Turkish Army was still there. Well, that was different. Turks are fascists. Yes; and it was forty-one years since the Soviet Union had gone in to assist the re-volution in Poland and Lithuania, and they are still there; eighteen years since they went to defend the revolution in Czechoslovakia; seven years since they went in to assist it in Afghanistan and . . .

I cannot remember at all how this conversation was brought to an end at last. It must have been Father Albert's achieve-ment. At any rate, they were suddenly all on their feet, not for an execution but because for the time being they had had enough of the game. Father Albert shepherded them out through the door, and the volunteer worker and I looked at each other as the occupants of some beleaguered *ksar* might have, taking in that the din had given way to silence, and looking between their mud crenellations to find that the enemy had incomprehensibly turned and galloped away.

Our problem, however, was still with us: I was an unac-ceptably dangerous guest for the priest. As soon as he came back I put it to him once more that I must leave immediately, while the chance existed. At no time had Father Albert seemed to be putting pressure on me. But now — still without pressure — he said very quietly: 'If you go tonight, then my life is in very great danger.' Things might be easier to arrange in the morning. Probably PLOTE had no further use for me; but gangs

25

from two other Eelamist parties were in the town. They were very jealous of each other, and each was afraid of the others picking up a potential prize. By the morning some of them, if not all, might have gone away and then the rest would probably lose interest, being no longer afraid of losing face. Under God this was at least a chance.

And so, like any random assembly of guests in a Greek mountain monastery, we went in to dinner, the priest having first called his sister, a sweet and self-effacing young girl, to take me to wash my face and hands and show me where I should presently sleep.

While we ate, we talked as we should have anywhere else. The old woman who had cooked the meal was perhaps a Hindu, or perhaps had been over-excited by the need to provide for two guests; at any rate she had added a small amount of egg to the main dish, though it was a Friday, so neither Father Albert nor Queen Elizabeth would touch it. Still, they may not have thought that eating it was wholly sinful, for they pressed it on the volunteer worker and me rather than see it wasted.

It was weighing very much on my mind that the deadline for my return to Anuradhapura was already past, and soon conclusions would be drawn. If anyone were to give the alarm — perhaps by a telephone or radio call to the army camp here — a patrol might be turned out to investigate, and lives would be lost. So after dinner when the volunteer worker got on his bicycle to go home I asked if there was a public telephone in the town. Yes. Would he, then, ring the rest-house in Anuradhapura and say simply that I had been delayed? Nothing more, no suggestion that all was not well nor mention of where I was: no word that the thugs, if it came to their knowledge, would object to. He shifted his feet uneasily. Then he said: 'For my life, I dare not go even one yard out of the way to my house.'

So much for 'liberation'.

*

26

I was ready to leave as soon as it was light but again there was a posse of armed thugs shouting in the compound. Father Albert went out to try to reason with them. This time he really did seem to be making headway. At nine o'clock, after more than two hours' talk, some sort of agreement had been reached and I saw that they were going away.

Father Albert called to me and said, 'Get into your car now and go, quickly, before they change their minds. They say that no one will interfere with you.' He pointed over the compound wall. 'You must turn left there, and go straight, and keep on that road, keep on it. If you do anything else they will think you are going to the army camp, and they will shoot. Keep on it and for God's sake, don't stop the car.' And he blessed me quickly.

It was a right-angled turn out of the compound gate on to the road. Before I had picked up speed there were fifteen or twenty men, armed and unarmed, blocking the way. I knew that I ought to keep my foot down and drive into them, but I could not do it. Within seconds they had seized the doors, were crammed against the bonnet, were on all sides. One who had wrenched open the driver's door prodded me with his gun and snarled the single word: 'Git.' The tone, the meaning, were what I had witnessed the day before in the compound. I saw red, now as then, and instead of getting out of his way gripped the steering-wheel with both hands to hold myself in place. He knocked me sideways and flung himself in on top of me, his whole weight on my stomach, his feet on top of mine on the pedals, his left elbow in my ribs as he drove her off. Another man was in the front passenger-seat, half sitting on my head, and two more in the back seats. I did not know it yet, but a fifth was clinging to the roof.

For the first few seconds I could think of nothing but how to remove this loathsome body from mine. It was loathing, not pain, that I felt. I knew that the most important thing was to see where we were going. The man in the left-hand seat shifted, letting me breathe. I got my head up a few inches and had a glimpse of a causeway, but it was not enough. We were going fast and swerving erratically. A lurch gave me a few more inches, and since I could not see out of the car I took stock of the weapons inside it. Security forces generally want to know what the enemy is armed with, and it had not occurred to me yet that I should not escape from this lot. There were two sub-machine-guns (I memorized their features and later learned that they were Stirlings), a Kalashnikov rifle, an old .303 service rifle with fixed bayonet. This seemed the most unpleasant item, and the likeliest to be used in the circumstances. Why else bring it?

The car came to a halt beside a small wood. The man with a Stirling in the back seat got out, exchanged friendly-sounding words with the others as if thanking them for a lift, and disappeared into the trees. A fifth man holding a Kalashnikov now skittered down off the roof and got inside. I thought that we must have been a conspicuous piece of traffic going through the town: by now a lot of people must know what had happened. That was one thing to the good, I supposed.

We were out in the country now, running roughly north, not on the road I had come in by. We had been going fast, lurching and swerving, and I had been puzzled that the horn had never once been sounded. Now that I could see a bit more I realized it was because the driver could not find it — not surprisingly since it had been disconnected from its proper place and linked up to a temporary button-switch low down on the steering column. I said nothing at first, hoping for a crash which would resolve the situation one way or another. But when passers-by had twice almost been hit I reached out and pressed the horn myself. I did not like to do it because it seemed almost collaborating with my captors, but I did not want someone other than them to be killed unnecessarily. The front passenger made a movement as if he were going to smash his gun down on my arm, but realized what I was at and checked it just in time. Pleased as a monkey at learning how to make a noise, the driver let me shift enough to get nearly clear of him and see out over the dashboard.

We now bowled along with enough root-tooting to show that they were not the least afraid of notice. I drew the conclusion that the army camp had no unit they could send out in pursuit (they could hardly not have been alerted), and this saved me from hoping for a rescue which would not come. I concentrated on details of the road, from which someone with a map, some day, would be able to tell where I had been taken.

We went down a twisting dirt road which ended at a large open space of bare ground, on one side of which stood a big building slightly like a football stadium. I memorized its shape, rough orientation, and roof construction — which might help to identify it from the air. On the other side of the open space, at the beginning of another track, was a hut made of wood and mud. This turned out to be our destination. The front of it was open, but screened from the track by a fence and hedge. Inside, it was divided into four sections: the first a shed-like store, the second an armoury, crammed full, the third, only about five feet wide containing a table, a bench, and a window three-quarters boarded up; and the fourth a kitchen. There were about fifteen men and boys here, armed and unarmed. I was put into the store and told to wait. The car was parked in front of the store, and its contents taken out and examined by everyone. I used this distraction to look into the next, armoury, section, thus learning what it was.

There was only one thing among my possessions which I was afraid of their finding, and that was the letter from the General. It was my death-warrant and I knew it, but there had been no chance to destroy it. I had it inside my spectacles-case, folded under the cleaning-cloth that opticians so thoughtfully supply.

After a few minutes I was moved into the narrow room with an armed youth to guard me. Soon an older man arrived, whom I named Ratface. My handbag, still on a strap from my shoulder, was taken and emptied out on the table, and Ratface began to examine its contents item by item, aided by the man who had driven the car.

It was the first time that I had had a proper look at the car-driver. He was probably twenty-five or twenty-six, with a terrorist-style moustache and bloodshot eyes. He reminded me of someone whom at first I could not place. Then it came back with startling clarity. The eyes were the eyes of Miles Gifford, the Cornish murderer, whom I had known when he was this age: an apparently simple, engaging, rugger-playing youth, who had lain in wait for his parents one night with an axe and killed them both, because they had said they would give him no more money. I had once seen Miles Gifford the worse for drink, with the killer's madness in his eyes: an unforgettable glimpse into an abyss. Now as I saw that look again in this new face I remembered a half-line out of Flecker's *Hassan*: 'As swans come double down a river, events come drifting double down our lives.' It seemed incongruous: what a pair of swans.

Now the questioning began, and two things soon became apparent. These people did not know anything about the techniques of interrogation. (Neither did I, but their ignorance was obvious even to me.) They had read pulp thrillers or (more likely) seen films purporting to show such things; but that is no basis for getting results in real life. And they had very little English. These two weaknesses were cards in my hand; and I needed them, for I had made some gross mistakes myself.

Picture a space about five feet wide by ten feet long, mud-walled and mud-floored; one end of a chipped wooden table pushed hard up against the end wall and just room for a narrow bench on each side of it. The car-driver, whom in my mind I called PK (for Pathological Killer), sat or more often stood at the far end on the left, fondling his gun. A nonentity was next to him, and then me. On the other side, Ratface was at the end, then a butter-fingered oaf with a Kalashnikov, then a lad of seventeen or eighteen, round-eyed and dreaming that this was real life. In the doorway spectators watched or passed and repassed; I had no attention to spare for them by now.

First my passport was studied. When had I arrived in Sri Lanka? They checked the entry stamp. And when had I left London? The day before. Triumph in the eyes: why had I not arrived on the day I left? Where had I spent the intervening day? I explained that on a sixteen-hour flight eastwards this difference of a day is not unusual or suspicious; but I could see that it had roused hopes in them of revelations to come. They found the entry and exit stamps from my visit in May. Why had I come? Where gone? Why come again? Then they found the entry stamp for September. Here was proof positive that I was a spy. 'Now we shoot you,' PK exclaimed with relish, levelling his gun on me. The nonentity in the middle of the bench slid out from between us and (understandably) never came back again. Ratface poured out a spate of questions, aimed to reach the same conclusion as PK's.

This charge of being 'a spy' was a fixation that would stay with them, simply because it was a necessary part in the play they were acting. I saw that common-sense considerations — what could there be to spy on in Mullaitivu church? — did not exist for them.

Ratface's English was too fast for PK, who hid his inability to follow it by seizing the passport and leafing through it again. Then he slammed it shut in triumph. 'When you come in Sri Lanka last time?'

'September 1985.'

'What date?'

I thought hard. 'About the 23rd, I think.'

'When you leave?'

'About October 16th.'

Up came the gun again. 'Do-on't lie to us.' (I cannot reproduce the dragging tone and concentrated menace with which both he and Ratface, and others later, used this phrase — as they did, over and over again, making it sound as savage as they could.) 'Entry visa, 23.9. *No exit visa!*' He riffled the pages. 'You are spy. Now we shoot you.' And the gun was up at my ear. I said: 'Look again. There's an exit stamp there.' But a horrible fear sprang into my mind. When I had left the island in October I had been seen off at the airport, together with some VIPs, by a senior member of the government; a functionary had taken all our passports and got them stamped while we sat in comfort with the champagne. Was it possible that one of the stamps had been omitted? I thought that it just could have happened. But it would do no good to say so: any contact whatever with the government, whether officially or at a personal level, was a capital offence to this crew. So I said confidently enough, 'Look carefully and you'll find it.' He went through the pages more slowly. 'No. Not here.' He and Ratface both began heaping abuse on me, and when PK brought his gun up to my head again Ratface nodded permission. They pushed me back against the wall. '*Now* we shoot you.' I was angry at their shilly-shallying and I had seen that they were not amenable to reason. I said, 'All right,' and shrugged a shoulder, deliberately indifferent; this wasn't bravado but because I could think of no better way to convince them that they were making fools of themselves. I waited. But now there were new sounds outside. Somebody had arrived, and they had to know who it was and expound their cleverness. By the time they came back the tension of the minute before had slackened. Ratface picked up the passport, thumbed through it, shoved it across to PK. I knew by their faces that they had found the exit stamp. They could not admit it, of course. It took them only moments to think of another line of attack.

'Hen you *leave London*?' None of these people could manage a *wh* in English, so their questions came out as 'Hen?' and 'Hair?', 'High?' and 'Hot?'

'January 10th.'

'Don't lie!' We were back in the same position again, triumph gleaming in the dark, bloodshot eyes. 'Hair is exit stamp from England?'

'Why should there be one? It's my country, I can leave it when I like.'

'You lie!' It was PK speaking. 'I know. I have British passport. They put stamp hen I come in, hen I go out.'

I said: 'You may have a British passport, but you're not English.' I was appalled that this horrible man should be free to come and go in my country as he pleased. It came to me suddenly that I knew whose hands I had fallen into. These were not properly speaking men at all, they were Kipling's *bandar-log*. Fragments of the story 'Kaa's Hunting' from *The Jungle Book* drifted across my memory like whiffs of a familiar scent: the mindlessness, the malice, the inability to hold on to an idea for half a minute at a time. The image was strengthened by a mental picture of the green baboon my godmother had had: the chattering laugh without lightness, the fingers endlessly picking to no purpose — as here on the trigger of the Kalashnikov — the puzzled, angry eyes. If they did not shoot me it would not be because of a rational decision, it would be because they had forgotten to. This discovery sent a surge of relief through me. Now that I knew what I was up against, I could manage better.

They were back at the contents of my handbag again by now, item by item, each scrap of paper studied by PK or Ratface, some by both, and I could see that often they could not read what they were holding but were not going to admit as much. That gave me yet more grounds for hope — dashed a few moments later when I saw among the scraps one that I had had no idea was there at all. It contained a list of notes for questions which I had been asking in the General's office.

'Naval Cdr. Trinco.

'Road to Pulmoddai: passable by Fiat?

'Use of word Sri and symbol?

'SEP — can I talk to?'

SEP: Surrendered Enemy Personnel. Even if I could think of something to account for the reference to the Naval Commander, those three initials would kill me. How on earth had I set off with that piece of paper on me? I clearly remembered taking it out the night before, with one or two others, and putting it — so I thought — with the things I was leaving behind in Anuradhapura. It is not curiosity that kills the cat, it is incompetence. What to do now?

I saw that they had put all the things out of the handbag in a heap between them, and that as they finished examining each one they put it on a separate pile, nearer to me. The two junior thugs on the bench beside Ratface watched, but they were interested in what their leaders lingered over, not what they put aside as finished. I kept my eyes on that potentially lethal scrap, and waited for my moment. It came when Ratface was scrutinizing one of several Foreign Exchange slips, and PK started to screw and unscrew my lipstick as if something were hidden in it. I reached out, pushed their pile a little closer to them, and palmed the incriminating scrap as I did so. I neither closed my fingers on it nor withdrew my hand, and when Ratface put the exchange slip down I took it from him, shoved it myself on to the 'finished' pile, and waited for him to discard the next piece. Two minutes later what I held in my hand was on the finished pile too, and well down in it, between three or four paper handkerchiefs.

But face had been lost over the passport, and I should have known that it would have to be recovered. Going through it again Ratface identified a Turkish stamp. What had I been doing in Turkey?

'Visiting friends.'

What did this long hand-written entry in Turkish mean? I translated it for them.

Who had paid for me to go to Turkey? No one pays for such journeys themselves (I think they thought that that was so). And then they turned the page and found a Jordanian visa. I knew at once that trouble was coming. The 'Eelam' groups work with the PLO, the PFLP, Libya and Syria. Jordan is an enemy in their eyes. What had I been doing there?

'Visiting friends.'

34

'Who are your friends?'

'The Australian Chargé d'Affaires in Amman and his wife.'

This time it was Ratface's gun that came up, and the narrow little eyes seemed running with venom and satisfaction. 'You are lying. Australia is not represented in Amman.'

'Yes it is.' I remembered that the Ambassador in Jordan covers Damascus too: Ratface had unwittingly told me that his organization had Syrian links. But now he was shouting at me. 'You lie! You are a dirty spy! Now we kill you!' They were both on their feet, snarling like curs on a garbage-heap, and I was against the wall again. I said: 'Go ahead then,' knowing that the smallest hint of giving way to them would nerve them to do it. And at that moment someone called from outside. Ratface said: 'Wait. We shall kill you,' and they both went out.

Outside I could see the boy with a Kalashnikov who was detailed to make sure that I stayed where I was, and beyond him five or six men standing round my car. The minutes slid by, and I thought that there were not many left for me. I remembered the poem I had started on the jungle road the day before, and wanted Tony to have it; so on the back of a shopping-list from the 'finished' pile I wrote it down, completing it as best I could in the time. For I thought there was a chance, however slender, that my few possessions might be found some day by some army patrol or the like, and so get back to him. I did not waste time supposing that I was going to get out myself; it was already plain enough to me that I should not.


The new arrival was clearly meant to impress me very much, in quite a new way. It was a girl guerrilla. She was dressed in something vaguely like a khaki uniform (all the others were in various mixtures of Tamil and European 'leisure' clothes) and she was so lamentably hideous that it was impossible not to feel sorry for her. I think she had been told to get me into

35

conversation and find out things about me; but she was too shy, and had too little English, to do it. So instead she told me she was twenty-six (I guessed that she had got into this *galère* because she was already irredeemably past the hope of marriage) and that the youth beside her was her younger brother, whom she had recruited into the band. She too sorted the contents of my handbag with a certain childlike pleasure, and finding a pocket comb in a plastic case (a present from an airline) she held it up in a puzzled way. 'Hot it is?' Looking at the matted stuff round her head I could understand her doubt. I began asking her the Tamil words for simple things: 'table', 'you', 'me', 'mother', and so on. When the others got back she was sent away, and I never saw her again, or any other female Comrade.

The others were disgruntled now, but something had given them a new, wholly illogical idea. There followed half an hour of questions aimed to trap me into an admission that I was an agent of MOSSAD, the Israeli Intelligence organization. When these questions had failed to elicit anything they fell back on plain accusations. Messing about with the 'finished' pile, Ratface came on the poem. For some minutes he was defeated by my writing, but at last he made out one line. 'Hot is written here?' he demanded. (He did not dare ask this about anything he had failed to read, for fear that I should lie to him and he not know it.) I read it: 'I go to greet my God today.' Up came the gun again, and there behind it the enraged interrogator's glare. '*Who* is your God?' For a second I could not imagine what he meant. These people were perfectly familiar with Christianity; some of them had quite likely been brought up as Christians themselves. Then in a flash I saw that he thought the words stood for a political leader. He thought he had stumbled on the proof that I was a 'spy'.

I forget what he said next, but we spent several minutes on this misunderstanding, I saying again and again, 'God is God. I have no other. God is not a man. Even people like you must know what the rest of us mean by "God".' At last it dawned

36

on him, and I have never seen on any face a look more loaded with frustration and rage and shock. Frustration at losing his triumph; rage because it is known that believers are unassailable; but shock? I saw that he was profoundly shocked because, although I was a woman in his power and virtually a dead woman already, a thing of no account, yet I was also the modern, western world of technology and advance, of everything enviable in capitalism. For someone in that world to believe in God was an act of treachery so unexpected that it knocked him off balance.

Seeing this on his face I felt hope rise again.


They left me for their midday meal. A child brought me a dish with some food on it, and since I was alone except for the man on guard outside the open doorway I used the time to look for possible escape routes. The wall facing me was made of mud up to about five feet. Above that were pieces of board tacked on to rough timbers and in one place near the top a piece of cardboard had been used to block a gap between wall joists and rafters. I thought that if I were alone and the sentry's attention distracted for a few minutes I might be able to pull myself up, dislodge that bit of cardboard without too much noise, and squeeze through into the space between the top of the wall and the palm-thatch roof. I should be over the armoury if this worked. I had seen cases stacked almost up to the roof against the wall. If there was room for me to wriggle in there they would hide me from below. When the apes came back to look for me it was a fair chance that they would search outside the hut instead of inside it, and I could lie doggo until dark, when there might be some chance of getting away. It was all pretty unlikely, I knew, but it was something to hold on by.

The food was not very edible, but I ate some, reminding myself that there was no guessing when or where the next meal would be.

*

When they came back they were in a state of high excitement and with a new interrogator, who began by telling me that I was now in the hands of the group called EROS. He took it for granted that I should know (and I did) that these letters stood for Eelam Revolutionary Organization of Students. His English was better than the others', and he launched straight in on a new line of attack, saying that he knew I was working for MOSSAD, and moving gradually over from accusations to questions. It was known, he said smoothly, that the government had allowed MOSSAD to set up an office in Colombo. Was it not true that it was in So-and-so Street? And similar questions, against all of which I woodenly (and truthfully) advanced total ignorance. There were one or two more physical threats during this, enough to keep me from getting over-confident. Then he began playing with the piles of paper and within seconds he had got to the scrap which I had transferred before. He spread it out and read it carefully, the other two watching with the intensity and fury proper to seeing that they had missed something, they had been tricked.

I felt the blood drain out of my face and limbs, rushing back not to the heart but to somewhere lower down, within the pelvic cradle. I thought that I must have changed colour like a chameleon does, and that they must notice it and know that they had got what they wanted at last. I began inventing answers to the questions that came thick and fast now. Yes, these were notes I had made about things I meant to do, and questions I wanted to ask, the day before yesterday. I had wanted to go from Anuradhapura to Trincomalee, and thence up the east coast to Pulmonnai. Why? Because it was a part of the island I hadn't seen before. Didn't I know the people there were Tamils? Yes, that was why I wanted to see it. Why had I written 'Naval Cdr'? Because I was told that only he could give me permission to go that way. And had he given it? No, I had not known how to contact him. But I had given up the idea, because someone in the car-hire office had told me the road from Trincomalee to Pulmonnai was not passable anyway, that a bridge or two bridges had been destroyed. That was why I had decided to go to Mullaitivu instead.

I could see that they did not believe any of this, but it contained just enough facts to confuse. And luckily for me they went off after the red herring of the word 'Sri', a highly emotive subject among Tamils but of no relevance whatever just now. I had jotted it down only because I had wanted at some time to satisfy idle curiosity about how it was used. Their buzzings around it gave me a few more minutes to think up what to say about the fourth note: 'SEP. Can I talk to?'

By the grace of God the first question gave me my cue.

'Who is SEP?' It was asked with all the menace and all the certainty of victory that the newcomer could put into it; but it told me that he did not know what the letters stood for. I said it was a man's name, a name I could not remember. I was not even sure that SEP was what I had written. Let me look. I took out my spectacles and put them on; examined it; put them back again. I had done this a dozen times in front of them, always leaving the case open, always letting them see that I was not anxious, there was nothing concealed there. (But all the while the General's letter lay there like a time-bomb.) They argued for two or three minutes about whether it was not obvious that I had written SEP, before they came back to the point. *Who* was this man whose name I claimed to have forgotten? But by now I had thought what I should say. He was an official of some kind in the Naval Commander's office, whose name I had been given, down the telephone from the car-hire office, as the person whom I should consult about the state of the road. I had not heard the name properly, and Sinhalese names are impossible for foreigners anyway. I had scribbled the three letters to give myself a notion of it: Senapa . . . something? Sepalla . . . something? I had forgotten it, but it had not mattered as I had heard the road was unusable anyway, so I had never bothered to try to ring him.

Little as I knew about Sinhalese names I knew I had heard only one beginning with Sep. I was gambling on my Tamil questioners having no Sinhalese either, and no ear for languages. And the gamble came off. They went on to other questions about other subjects. But I knew that a residue of suspicion still lay there, and would not melt.

Quite suddenly the newcomer lost patience. There was a grunting exchange between him and Ratface and PK, then they were shouting at me again that I was a filthy spy for Israel and they would kill me. PK made to back me up against the wall again but the newcomer gave a jerk of the chin and said, 'Outside.' I guessed he was thinking of where blood would matter least. I thought I would rather walk out than let them get their hands on me. I stood up. And at that moment the roar of a motor-bicycle sounded from the track. 'Wait,' the newcomer said, and he went out, followed a moment later by the other two. Ratface as he passed said, 'We come back, we kill you.'

I stood waiting; then I thought: I'm not going to let these people think I care what they do. So to make the point clear I lay down on the bench and shut my eyes, as if I were taking an afternoon siesta.

I thought that I had probably got ten to fifteen minutes to live, and had better make the best use I could of them. It was not likely the poem would ever reach Tony, but it struck me as just possible that, if I wrote him a letter containing nothing that could possibly upset these people, and addressed it, and gave it to them to read and asked them to send it, they might do so. Might. It was a very small chance but, however small, worth trying for. I must know exactly what I was going to write and keep it very short, and write it very quickly. They would not wait.


Dr Johnson was right about the concentration of the mind. I had no difficulty whatever in deciding what I wanted to say. I

40

wrote the letter in my head as I lay on the bench with my eyes shut; I said that I loved him, and should go on doing so when I was dead in the same way as now (this had become completely clear to me) and that I knew he loved me and this made it possible. I asked him to tell the two children how much I loved them, and that I would have written to them too if there had been time: this one letter was for them too. I asked the three of them to love each other and stick together through thick and thin. And I asked Tony to marry again, for their sakes and his.

I had just got this completed in my head when I heard a faint scuffing close by. It was hesitant, not like Ratface and the others. I opened my eyes. One of the youngest of the gang (he looked about fourteen) had crept in and laid beside me a small bunch of bananas. A shaft of pleasure shot through me, that this simplicity and humanity still existed here; and I wanted to laugh too, because it so strongly recalled all those stories about the condemned man's last breakfast. I have always thought of a banana for breakfast as a great luxury. I ate one, thinking how good life is after all. Then I lay down again and prayed.

Odd as it may seem, I did not pray to be reprieved: 'God, get me out of here.' I had brought this situation on myself, blamed no one else for it, and would take what came. What I really wanted was strength to go through with it properly. I was fairly certain that I could stand still and wait for the shot, and keep my eyes open and my mouth shut. But I wanted desperately to think about Tony during the last few seconds; and I knew that if I did, tears would come. It is a weakness I have suffered from all my life, that if I am moved I cannot keep them back. And the apes would misread them. They would think I was weeping from fear, and that would give them a huge, lewd pleasure, the very one, probably, that had turned them to this trade. I would not give it to them. So I prayed to God for strength to hold the tears in, because I could not bear to forgo my thoughts.

*

41

Soon they came back, and I got up again to walk out and be murdered. But their heads were full of questions once more. Human nature is incurably optimistic and before long I began to think that things might yet fall out right, though it was difficult to see how, once they had let me see and hear so much. I was in better fettle for them now, because I felt fairly sure I could make a go of dying. However, there was still a precaution to be taken. I knew that in circumstances of this kind people may lose control of their natural functions; and the pleasure they might get from seeing me weep would be nothing to the kick that would give them. So the next time they broke off and went outside for one of their powwows I walked after them and up to PK, who had been left on guard, and asked for the girl.

'She is gone. Hy you want her?'

I said: 'Woman.'

'No woman.' Then he understood. 'You want . . .?' He did not know what to say but made a vague gesture — not an obscene one.

'Yes. Where should I go?' They had had me for six hours or more now, so it must seem a reasonable request.

He laughed in an embarrassed way and said, 'We use open air.'

That was what I had expected and hoped. I said: 'Right. You call the boys this side; I go that side.' I pointed towards the back of the hut. Seeing he was about to refuse, I touched my watch and added: 'Two minutes.' He hesitated, then nodded and called out to the others, beckoning with his free arm. When he had got them together I walked through the kitchen and out at the back of the hut.

There was a patch of long grass and weeds, growing two and a half or three feet high, and I thought for a moment that this gave straight into a belt of jungle, seventy yards or more away. But a second glance showed a wire fence across it half-hidden by weeds growing through and into the mesh. At either end of the hut were fences, and bare ground beyond them.

I was certain that, though good manners were being observed, someone with a rifle was still watching me; and I had only got two minutes. The grass was too thick and high to run in, and the fence would take vital seconds to get over. They might all be very bad shots, but they could hardly all miss at the distance. But while I dealt with what I had come out for I took very careful note of angles and distances. For I thought, if I can keep the game of questions and answers going until dark, then I can make this same request again, and they'll think it's all right because it was all right before; and I'll crawl through the grass — they won't be able to see it waving in the dark — and I'll be over the fence and into the jungle before they know I've started.

I knew it would not really be as easy at that, but I could see that it offered a better chance than that bit of cardboard up against the roof, and my spirits lifted disproportionately.

When I got back into the hut the inquisitors were still outside. I took a quick look at the duty sentry, saw that his mind was not on his job, and with my back to him took the General's letter out of my spectacles-case and slipped it inside my shirt. I did not (still do not) know why I did this, and a moment later I thought that it had been a very stupid move. But it was too late to change it again.

The powwow now going on outside was of a new kind, with a new participant. Earlier in the day a boy had been brought because he had more English than the others; but he had disappeared again and I had forgotten him. Now he had reappeared and some plan was being discussed. They shovelled the contents of my handbag back into it and pushed it towards me. But just as I was going to take it the newcomer reached out and took my spectacles-case out of my hand. He opened it, took out the specs, examined them, squinting through the lenses (I think he had thought they might be fakes, a disguise). Then he took out the cleaning-cloth and looked underneath. I felt the General's letter stiff against my skin, and kept my arm loosely across my chest in case an outline should show. The newcomer slid the specs into the case again, snapped it shut, handed it back to me. My heart-beat thudded under the letter.

Now everyone got to their feet. I was taken outside and put into the Fiat, with PK driving and two others, armed, in the back. We set off by a different road from the one we had come in by. I hardly thought what might happen next: I was too busy noting landmarks and directions. I could hardly believe my luck that they were letting me see where we were going. We went to a house on the outskirts of a jungle village, and it was explained to me that the English-speaking boy's family lived there. It had been decided that I must be interrogated further tomorrow, and I could not be left at the hut overnight; so these people had been made responsible for me. They would have to answer for it if I was not there for questioning in the morning. Then I was pushed through the gate and they drove off.


They kept me for three days in the jungle village. I was under no physical constraint: I could have walked away at any time. But others would have paid the price if I had, and that is the strongest of all deterrents. When I asked what they meant to do they said they were waiting for instructions from the north; then for a 'leader' who was coming down to see me for himself. I shall not describe those days in detail, except for one incident which provided light relief. Towards the end of the second afternoon two middle-aged Tamils in semi-European clothes appeared: dark-complexioned, stout, benevolent-looking men, carrying copies of the Old Testament. They were Jehovah's Witnesses touring the jungle villages, there to read and expound parts of the Bible to whomever would listen. They had the text in English with Tamil translations. They sat down in the house and held a kind of class; and when it was over it was explained to them that I was here while decisions were being taken elsewhere, and that I should probably be shot.

They were saddened by this news and urged me to read the Seventy-first Psalm, which I should find consoling. I had no idea what it was, but said that if there were any choice I would prefer the Twenty-third. Did I mean the Twenty-second? they asked. No, the Twenty-third. They shook their heads, saying that yes, it too was good, but in my particular circumstances I should find No. 71 the most suitable. They looked it out and gave it to me, and I read: '. . . Deliver me in thy righteousness, and cause me to escape: incline thine ear unto me and save me . . . Deliver me, O my God, out of the hand of the wicked, out of the hand of the unrighteous and cruel man.' They prayed for me, and later went away again through the jungle, walking delicately, like Agag. But as far as I know they told no one where I was.

On the third afternoon the leader from the north arrived. He was an unimpressive figure and I cannot now remember what I called him. He and his henchmen spent half an hour desultorily asking questions; then I heard the distinctive labouring stutter of the Fiat's engine in the distance and we went out to the jungle track, where presently it appeared with PK at the wheel. I was ordered to get in. What for? I asked. The leader (he was not a leader of much, I think) said that I was to be taken to Jaffna. I had told my interrogators that I knew a Tamil literary figure there, a Professor N. They said this was an obvious lie, so they were going to confront me with him. If he should confirm that he knew me he would presumably ask them to let me go, and they would do so; but he would of course deny me and they would then carry out the execution which they had a perfect right to, now.

I was clearly meant to understand this as an example of mercy and justice combined. I did not see it so, but it filled me with hope because I believed what they said, and as the Professor did know me, and might possibly not be too scared to say so, I thought that I now had a chance. So I got into the

Fiat with a light heart. Two armed baboons got in behind me and we wobbled away down the track, one baboon with the muzzle of his rifle sticking out of the window and the other keeping his in the rough direction of my head.

We drove north by jungle tracks and secondary roads, at speeds rarely above 25 m.p.h. and often down to two or three. PK could only just drive the car, and knew nothing about it, but fell into accepting my advice as to when to change gear, what pot-holes to steer round, and which to grind into and out of. A day earlier I should have kept my mouth shut and let him come to grief, but now I was getting hour by hour nearer to the professor.

Our route took us across farming land and through villages. We had started in the late afternoon; as the shadows lengthened men and women were coming home from the fields, or gathering in the village streets. I watched to see how they would take the strange sight we presented: these armed men with their weapons very much in evidence (they kept them in plain view through the villages) with their obvious captive a white woman, an odd enough sight up here anyway. (In the jungle village little silent crowds had gathered at the garden fence to stare at me, and the English-speaking boy had said: 'Some of these have never seen a white face before.') By now there would have been at least local newspaper or radio reports of a kidnapping, so many of them could guess what they were seeing. I was not naïve enough to imagine that anyone would dare try to intervene, or to get word out of our passing, to anyone in authority. Terrorist control is established and maintained by ruthless punishment of anyone who shows the smallest tendency to interfere or to talk. But I had seen enough in other countries to know the difference between places where the men with guns are seen as friends and are welcome, and where they are dreaded and endured. In no village we went through now was there any smile for them – and no country has a more readily smiling population than Sri Lanka. No hands went up in greeting; there was no waving or excitement even from children, who in such places will normally run behind and alongside a car like leaves in the wind, laughing and shouting. Nor were there silent stares. All eyes were turned to the ground as we passed. It was as if we were a funeral cortège. So much for the myths about popular devotion to 'the boys'.

I had time now, too, to think about my own relations with them. These people would release or kill me without the remotest reference to anything that had passed between us, so any appearance of friendship could only be delusion. And I was going to lie to them, and fool them, exactly as much as I needed to; what sort of friendship then could I offer? It would be a cheap fraud.

'Petrol,' said PK, interrupting my train of thought. 'How many miles?'

'D'you mean, how many miles can we go with what we've got?'

He thought for a minute. 'No.'

'How many miles to one gallon?'

'Yes.'

'On a good road, thirty-five, thirty-nine. Like this,' (we were weaving along a cratered track at under 10 m.p.h. in second gear) 'twenty-five.'

He looked puzzled and rather upset. 'I thought, fast speed, more petrol?'

'Low gear, more petrol.'

'Oh . . . I change up?'

I thought, how can I feel enmity towards this inept beginner? And then: yet he'll shoot me without compunction if I try to jump out of the car. Real life is endlessly interesting.

Not for the first time I thought about the story of Julius Caesar and the pirates. Caesar was a bargaining-chip, worth so many sesterces. I was a bargaining-chip worth — well, nothing at all. And most determinedly I was going to go on concealing from them *why* I was worth nothing: because of the letter which I had left behind with the General.

47

It must have been nearly midnight when we stopped at last. The moon showed a fence of cane-stalks with a gate in it, whence a short path across rough ground led to a large, apparently unfinished bungalow: the windows seemed to be still boarded up and a huge pile of bricks lay at one corner. We groped round to the side furthest from the road, where one of the baboons produced a key and tried it in a big, low double door, without result. The three of them then quarrelled and abused each other, and finally one went round the house and found another door which the key did fit. Inside we were in pitch darkness until someone found an oil lamp and lit it. Only two rooms seemed to be accessible. The outer one contained a table, a bench, a chair, and a pile of bedding. The inner one lay behind the door we had failed to open; the lamp now showed massive metal bolts on the inside. It contained nothing at all except a broken bed. But to my vast relief PK pointed to this, said, 'You, here,' and retreated with the other two, taking the lamp with him. I heard the door being locked.

The next morning I sized the place up as best I could, although I supposed we should not be here for long. The house was unfinished and unfurnished, and was probably meant to stay so. The room where PK and the others had spent the night had a proper front door, facing south-east with a porch to shade it, a window on each side of this, and a window facing south-west, towards the road. All three windows were of frosted-glass, with stout iron grilles on the inside.

The room where I had slept was long and narrow, and the right-hand long wall was mostly taken up by the locked doors I had seen from the outside last night. Inside, they had heavy bolts. A piece of string was tied across the doors, and supported a line of terrorists' washing: shirts, two or three sarongs neatly folded, black-and-yellow striped underpants. (I wondered if these had been chosen as suitable for 'tigers'.) On the opposite side of the room (the inside wall) was another pair of double doors, handsomely carved, as if they were the doors into some senior functionary's sanctum. They were furnished on this side with bars, locks and bolts of solid brass, all secured, and the main bolt had a padlock on it too. The bed stood against the short wall forming the end of the room, and there was a window above it, high up and heavily boarded.

Alongside the door from the front room into this one was an opening into a tiny peasant kitchen: a brick hob (on which fires of sticks are lighted), a shallow sink with a plug-hole but no waste-pipe; a bucket (no pipe or tap), a ewer, and a brick shelf bearing a box of matches, a piece of grimy soap, a razor and one or two other small things. This kitchen had its own outer door, which PK had by now unlocked. It gave on to a piece of rough ground littered with planks and builders' mess. Fifty yards away stood a privy made of new concrete. It faced the house and had no door, but there was a piece of board which could be propped up to provide partial cover. Long, high fences ran down the sides of this piece of ground, and at the bottom of it, perhaps 150 yards away, was a round, mud-and-straw peasant hut, out of which naked children now and then toddled before a larger child retrieved them. I never saw an adult there.

Outside the kitchen door was a well with a rope and bucket but no windlass. I hauled some water up hand-over-hand and washed. To do this under armed guard refreshes as it would anywhere else, but is not relaxing.

PK brought me a bowl of food, and I asked when we should be going on to the Professor. Soon, he said, and went away. Time wore on immensely slowly. In the jungle there had been distractions of one kind and another; here there was nothing at all. There were two guards on duty in PK's absence: a trainee whom I called Tiger Tim because he was like a huge armed child, and one whom I now can remember little or nothing about, so I shall call him the Third Man, for convenience. Tiger Tim was about eighteen. He looked innocent and friendly and at the same time innocently brutal. He clearly

49

worshipped PK, and would have done anything he was told, whether it might be to clean the prisoner's shoes or wring the prisoner's neck. He was much lighter-coloured than the others, with a big, flattish, rather likeable face, a bit pock-marked. He laughed easily. The mental instability so plain in PK was perceptible in Tiger Tim too, but on a much slower fuse. Probably it had not yet flowered.

The Third Man looked to be in his middle twenties. He seemed to be reckoned of inferior status to the other two, and was left to do the chores.

I made a detailed map of the place in my mind, registering especially those details that would be recognizable from the air: shape and area of roof; distances and angles between house and road, privy, thatched hut. When midday came I oriented my map by the direction of the sun, and drew the whole thing into a doodle on the back of a paying-in slip in my cheque-book.

Two oversights by my captors were of very great value to me. In all their questionings and hectorings they never took away from me a tourist road-map of the island which I had had in the car and had managed to scoop into my handbag. With its aid I had learned where I had been in the jungle. I could not place this house because the last few hours' drive, in the dark, had been directionless for me. But early this morning I had heard a train pass, not far away. I tried to guess the angle of the line to the road outside and to my north-south axis: it became possible to see where I must be, to within a fairly small area. I thought this important because I was by now fairly certain that the house contained a biggish dump of arms; hence the barricading off of two-thirds of it, the fortress-like locks and bolts, the wide doors (for loading and unloading) and the thoroughness of the boarding-up of the windows. The unfinished building work would provide good cover. Lorries could come in and out; and the high fences completely shut out prying eyes. I wanted badly to be able one day to identify where this place lay.

My tormentors' other great error was in leaving me my watch. They had examined it of course, but it was of no interest to them, being of the cheapest kind, much inferior to their own. But it kept time with the astonishing accuracy that modern watches have attained; it showed the date, which for some reason is a major help to keeping prisoners sane; it did not have to be wound, so the information on it was not dependent on me. And it enabled me, as watches do, to get roughly accurate compass directions. Since all travellers are potential kidnap victims today, I would offer this advice to everyone: never leave home without a digital watch too cheap and commonplace to be desirable.


I am not clear in my mind about how long I spent in the arms-dump house: two nights, perhaps three. And I have lost the sequence of events.

It was here that PK spoke about discos, asking me suddenly if I found it hard not to go to one every night. I couldn't help it, I burst out laughing and said: 'At my age?' At once he brought the gun-barrel round on to me, his face suffused with fury: not a pleasant sight. He began to shout at me that he knew everything about English life; he had been to England many times and was not to be fooled. All the women go to discos, whatever their age; all are immoral; all the men take their pay or their hand-outs straight to the pubs and spend the money on drink. All the young without exception are on drugs — a particularly despicable vice in his view — as well as drink, and the girls think of nothing day and night but sex with anyone they can get their hands on. They are worse than trash from top to bottom.

I tried in the mildest way to suggest that there are a few areas of England, especially away from the big cities, where life is not exactly like this; but his anger mounted dangerously.

51

It was not the subject that was infuriating him, it was that I had laughed at him, and the implication that he might have got something wrong. I saw that he not only wanted to believe in the truth of what he was saying, he *did* believe it. This made me think about what he could actually have seen of English life. He sputtered and ranted on, and the answer that gradually emerged was: the clientele of pubs and clubs in south-east London, people who no doubt saw themselves as advanced, and who liked to play up to 'revolutionaries', how-ever little they might know about the subject. No doubt they had thought they were impressing him and his kind favourably with their modern, daring, reckless approach to life. But instead, their views had disgusted him. He said that he had been four times to Moscow and East Berlin, also to Prague and Sofia, and that these places were vastly preferable to London. Why? Because the women in socialist countries were decent and didn't go round naked and behaving like stray bitches. Real Communists couldn't endure such conduct.

That was not a good afternoon. Psychopaths are easily upset, and I had upset him. Furthermore I was alone with him: the other two had been sent off on some errand. The atmo-sphere changed and became prickly with menace, imprecise but unmistakable. The almost total absence of furniture made it difficult to put distance between us inconspicuously. He went away, came back, took a tube of ointment out of his pocket and put it on the table, sliding it furtively half-behind an empty lemonade-bottle. Then he went through into the inner room, shutting the door behind him. The tube was of a lubricant cream made by the German pharmaceutical company KY. I spent the next few minutes examining how the iron grilles were fastened over the windows; but a thorough job had been made of it. I reminded myself that the most marked character-istic these people had shown me so far was their bird-brained volatility. Anything would distract them, the hottest trail might be abandoned for the lightest reason or none at all. There would be some simple way of diverting PK when he reappeared. And then I heard voices, and the key turning in the lock of the outer door. Tiger Tim and the Third Man were back. I had not until this moment visualized feeling grateful to any of these people for their presence.

It had become clear that most of this gang's ideas (if the word 'ideas' was applicable to them) derived from Mao Tse-tung's rules of conduct for guerrillas, filtered through Guevara and Regis Debray. These include very strict instructions on conduct: no stealing, no mishandling of women, and so forth. There appeared to be not much camaraderie between them, but a good deal of carping or censorious supervision one of another; so I thought I could assume that so long as two or three of them were gathered together Mao's rules would not be seriously broken. It was therefore reassuring to have read them.

The next morning when I was at the well Tiger Tim came up and offered me a loan of the communal soap. Then he said shyly: 'You want –' he had hardly any English, but rubbed two fists together – 'wash clothes?'

I said: 'I have no others.'

'We have.' And he went and took from the indoor washing-line-cum-wardrobe a clean check shirt and a sarong and held them out to me. I didn't know how to make the sarong stay up. 'Like this,' he said, demonstrating on himself. So I went back indoors and put on the terrorists' clothes, then washed my own by the time-honoured method of spreading them on one stone and beating them with another. I hung them on the vacant line above the well, in hope that a helicopter might go over us and its pilot might spot them and recognize that they were not local. For helicopters did go over quite often. That morning, when I asked yet again when we were going to reach Professor N., PK had answered, 'It is very dangerous; we are very near Elephant Pass.' Elephant Pass is a causeway, the only land link between the Jaffna Peninsula and the rest of the island. This geographical oddity is the reason why the terrorists have been able to get a grip of the Peninsula: it is a natural island fortress. The causeway is just wide enough to carry a road and a single-track railway line, close together; on either side lies a wilderness of lagoons and sand-spits and reedy marshes. The terrorists have their own routes through these. The army holds the causeway and a piece of gravel beach which provides a landing-pad.

Thus I left my clothes on the line as a kind of signal-flag, knowing there was at least a chance that it might be read; I hoped PK would forget about them. And so he did for several hours, until his voice was drowned by the chunter of a helicopter coming up on a line that would pass almost due over us. Then he dived out like a conger from its hole and snatched them down. He did not seem to have guessed that I had hung them there on purpose, but he had the manner of a junior who fears a reprimand if something gets known. I thought that the house was meant to appear unoccupied: hence the internal drying-line and the absence of electricity.

In the afternoon Ratface appeared briefly and said we should be on our way as soon as dusk fell. Thinking about Elephant Pass I asked how we would go, and he replied, 'By ferry' — or so I thought. I knew that before the trouble started there had been ferries across the lagoons, but I had not heard that any was still operating now; and if it were, it would be only for the sake of supplies to the civilian population, so it would be under police or army supervision. I could see no way in which this crew could get me aboard unnoticed.

However, I was a good deal cheered by the thought that we should before long be under way again towards the Professor. Release might easily be only a day away.


About 5 o'clock Ratface was back. I put my own clothes on again (in that steamy climate drying is a slow business without wind, so they were still very wet) and was taken outside. I used the few minutes while the others were locking up to register details of the outside of the house and what lay round it; then we were out in an empty road, and there waiting for us was not the Fiat any more but a small farm tractor. PK mounted beside the driver, Ratface behind him, Tiger Tim and the Third Man, one over each wheel; and I was put on a folded sack at the rear, facing backwards with my feet dangliing or hitched up on the towing-bar.

A few biggish thunderheads of cloud were building up in the north and east: there would be rain later. But for the most part the sky was clear, stars coming out at random, a little cluster at a time, like party-goers with a long evening ahead of them. I thought (wrongly) that I had solved one puzzle: the word I had mistaken for 'ferry' must have been 'Fergie'. It was a Ferguson tractor that we were on. I thought that they were exaggerating in using it; for the first hour and a half we came on no obstacle that I could not have coaxed the Fiat through, or over, if I had been allowed the wheel. But of course I should not have been allowed it.

All this was lush farming land, paddy and corn and cane, with water running in innumerable channels and the land almost as flat as the sea. We stopped at a small village where they bought supplies and took on petrol. Everyone seemed very glum and it all took a long time. There seemed to be a lot of questions in the air, but no one actually asked them. Then we got on board and were off again. There were no more villages after this, but there were labourers, men as well as women, going home, and farmers driving other tractors. No one greeted the baboons, who still kept their four guns bristling; one or two men stared in silence after us. Whenever I could get a glimpse of the Pole Star I took a line on our direction, but we were running roughly north so it was mostly behind my head.

At last we reached an end of made tracks, and there was nothing but reeds and shingle and thick black mud, and rice running wild. We bucketed up and down across ditches and nullahs, and once nearly overturned; they all giggled with excitement. A short heavy rainstorm came on. It was clear that

55

they felt very daring, though they seemed to be exposed to no danger. Finally we mounted a low mud ridge and came out on to a long smelly beach. I thought that I could dimly make out a further shore, I guessed half a mile away, but I knew that in this light I could be sure of nothing. PK said: 'Now we take ferry.'

It was now 9 o'clock. The rain had thinned away and we could see well enough by a milky, diffused moonlight. PK and Ratface produced torches and stood at the water's edge, flashing signals, but no answering flash came back. 'He is late,' said PK. 'He is never late,' said Ratface. The Third Man picked up a crab and offered it to me. Ten minutes went by; twenty; they were signalling like demented glow-worms, but there was no response. Gloomily they gave orders to the Third Man, who fetched a basket from the tractor and distributed hard-boiled eggs, curry-balls, and oranges to us all, then bottles of pop. I was conscious of sharp embarrassment in PK and Rat-face: their staffwork had broken down, on their first op-portunity to display it. Ratface confided that there was a boatman over there whose duty it was to come across for them at any time when they signalled. But after 10 o'clock it was certain he would not come; he would be afraid. Of what? I wondered. There were no security forces up here, and in any case they did not operate by night.

Finally Ratface said: 'No good. We must go back.' My heart sank. Up till now I had been enjoying this expedition. A ride on a tractor is always fun, and the circumstances of this ride had given it an extra flavour. But the thought of going back, of another night in that horrible house, another endless day's waiting for dusk, and then perhaps the same checkmate again because it was too late, was almost more than I could bear. I thought that they must have some surer means of com-munication than this. I said: 'How do you usually go?'

PK said, 'Ourselves? We walk.'

I said, 'All right. I can walk too, so why go back?' And as he seemed unconvinced: 'Come on: let's start.'

He said: 'Can you walk upon the water?'

That was rather a facer. I said, 'No, but I don't think you can, either.' Ratface joined the conversation and it became clear that what was meant was wading. I asked how deep the water was. From about here to here, they said, touching above the knee and then near the hip-bone. And how long did the crossing take? How long actually in the water?

'It takes us two hours.'

That seemed a tall order, but the thought of going back was worse and besides, pride was telling me that if they could do it I would show them that I could too. I said again, 'All right: come on.'

'You think you can?'

'I can try.'

'And if you can't?' said PK.

'Then you'll help me.'

They laughed so much that I thought they were going to drop their AK47s in the water. 'I *help* you?' PK gasped. Never in his life had he heard anything so exquisitely funny as the idea that he might help anyone. 'I *help* you?' Ratface patted him on the back, and the Third Man began to laugh too, and brought him another curry-puff.

But when order had been restored they decided more soberly not to try it. 'You see,' Ratface said, 'we have orders to get you there. We cannot risk any accident.'

With a leaden heart I went back with them to the tractor and we boarded it again and set off. Freedom had seemed only a few hours away. And now?

The rain had made the going even worse than before, and we tilted and slithered and plunged along with the tractor wheels throwing up liquid mud in showers and dollops the size of cowpats. After about two miles they pulled off behind a long, feathery hedge and turned in to a well-screened farmyard.

Lanterns were brought, two young boys appeared, rubbing sleep out of their eyes and wildly excited by our arrival, then slowly, with both bewilderment and reluctance, an old couple. Nothing was plainer than that they wanted no part in this; but they were under orders. The old woman was sent off to make tea, and while the old man muttered in the background, the boys spread out on the concrete floor the cotton covers they had been sleeping in. The terrorists sat down.

The farmhouse took up all one side of the yard, and consisted of a kind of veranda raised about a foot above ground level, giving access behind it to a big store and two or three little tunnel-like rooms. The veranda would hold Ratface and the rest, but what to do with me?

The two boys were drunk with wonder and admiration at the weaponry displayed in front of them, their eyes as big as jerboas'. Ratface had acquired an M16 the day before, and was showing it off as if he had designed it himself, or at least captured it — which he had not. It was passed from hand to hand with reverent delight, until one lad almost dropped it — Ratface catching it in the nick of time before it hit the concrete. Everyone looked shocked, and Ratface repossessed it with a schoolmaster's severity and brought the party to an end.

The old lady beckoned me over to a door and indicated that behind it was where I should sleep. The room inside was scarcely more than a cupboard, crammed to the ceiling with junk, one wall taken up by a collapsing bedframe piled with rags. I realized it was her own bed, and demurred, but she insisted, and Ratface came over and gave orders to the same effect.

I was so thickly coated in mud that I was not prepared to lie down on anyone else's rags, however lowly. I was not the old lady's prisoner, I was her guest. I said that I must wash. There was a well about fifty yards away, behind the house: further than I could be trusted on my own so PK and Tiger Tim came with me with their Kalashnikovs. Here too there was no windlass, and the bucket was large and the rope very

58

long. I felt suddenly exhausted and conveyed that one of them should do the hauling. PK took both rifles and Tiger Tim rather reluctantly let the bucket down. When he had got it back brimming on the parapet I thought, as well be hanged for a sheep as a lamb; any child in Greece would know how to do this for someone else. So expanding speech with gestures I showed him how to sluice the water over my arms and legs and head while I washed down. He was sullen at first, no doubt thinking it *infra dig*; then he began to giggle. PK decided to wash some mud off too, and he too began giggling. The whole thing became an hilarious joke, and for some minutes the three of us staggered about in the moonlight throwing water over each other and roaring with laughter. At last the two men began washing each other, and I left them and walked back towards the house. Fifty yards: could I make a successful break for it in that distance? Probably I should not get far, but that was not what mattered. I had this chance because I had got them to trust me; by the same token I could not take it. It would be like breaking parole – or any other form of breaking one's word. Tomorrow would be another matter: we should be enemies again, kidnappers and captive, and anything would be permissible. But tonight I had myself called a truce. It was not for me to break it.


The next day was a difficult one, the farm people terrified, the terrorists edgy, and everyone tired. At right angles to the farmhouse a second house had been built, mainly of mud and palm-thatch, for the old couple's married son and his family. The two men took their own tractor and went out early. The women as they carried on with their chores did their best without a syllable of common language to make me feel at home. Ratface did not allow me off the stoep, but they made me sit in the only chair. It was the old man's place of honour, an upright wooden affair inexplicably fitted with a hinged table across the arms, like a baby's. They brought a portable radio, tuned it to a hideous jangle, turned it up as loud as possible, and set it beside me. I did not dare show pain, because they seemed to be enjoying it and I thought it was probably a treat to them, ordinarily reserved for the boys. A troop of small children kept peeping round corners, as terrified of me at first as if I had been an iguanodon. I played finger-games for them, Ladders and Here's-the-church and the like, until they could do them too. But it is very difficult to kill a whole day by such means.

PK had hidden the tractor inside the storeroom at the back of the stoep, and the four of them stayed mostly inside, tinkering with it, while whoever remained on guard over me kept well back out of sight. I wondered whom these precautions were taken against. There were no security forces within miles; there had never been any attempt to control territory from the air; and if any pilot had spotted a man or a tractor about a farmyard he could not have thought that there was anything wrong in that. So they could only be hiding from the local Tamil population whom they claimed to be liberating; or else from a rival gang of liberators. Or they were simply enraptured by the mannerisms of the clandestine life. I felt very sad for the old couple. They were being badgered and bullied about their own home by their uninvited guests, and they would lose to them the two young men, already visibly and helplessly in love with the power of the gun.

At last sun and tide were thought low enough, the tractor was brought out again, and we were off — no earlier than before but with only half an hour's ride to do instead of two hours'. And again I watched the arrogance and self-admiration with which my captors displayed themselves and their armed might, and the silence with which workers coming in from the fields turned away from them.

Last night the shore had looked dark and muddy, the prospect uninviting. Muddy it still was, but it lay now in a landscape of radiant, pristine beauty. Perhaps half a mile away across the water from us a low island, scarcely more than a sandbank tufted with green, made a thin sliver on the surface. PK said that the ferryboat would be waiting there. The further shore of the lagoon was scarcely visible at all: I thought it must be two to three miles away.

I took off my sandals and waded into the water. It was hard going because our feet sank into mud up to the ankles and the tide was only just low enough: we were well up to the thighs. The temperature was like new milk, and that, together with the shortness of the distance, made me think it was going to be easy; but it took us half an hour to reach the island, and well before that I had begun to stagger from tiredness and finally keeled over into the water. The others had been striding happily ahead, safe in the knowledge that here there was no risk at all of my being able to make a run for it, and doubtless glad not to have the bother of watching. But hearing me flounder and splash PK looked back — and then a truly astonishing thing happened. He thrust his rifle into Tiger Tim's hands — the first time I had seen him let go of it — came wading back as fast as he could go, hauled me on to my feet, all but wrung me out, seized my leather handbag off my shoulder, checked that my passport had not fallen out of it, hung it round the Third Man's neck, and for the rest of the way held on to me by one arm. As we plodded towards the islet he seemed to be almost in a trance. He had *helped*, was helping. I think the reality seemed as incredible to him as the suggestion had, the night before.

But I was grateful for the lesson I had learned in the moonlight walking back from the well: that a prisoner can give no room to compromise. Accept the most transient moment of friendship and you lock the handcuffs on your own wrists. The users of modern terrorism must know this all too well, so they are delighted to encourage victims with the idea of saving themselves through the discovery of sympathy with their captors.

*

The sand-spit islet was bigger than it had looked, and on its further side, screened by reed and tamarisk scrub, lay the ferry. That is, a man in a loincloth stood up to his shins in the shallows holding a fathom of rope to which were made fast two logs some eight feet long, loosely hitched together. On these I was told to sit, roughly amidships, and the leather briefcase in which the terrorists apparently carried their documents was given to me to hold between my knees. PK took his seat behind me, with his Kalashnikov as usual not very far from the back of my neck, the ferryman took the tow-rope over his shoulder, and we glided off with the other two wading behind us. Ratface stayed on shore.

Then began a two-hour journey which is among the most magical that I have ever made. Water and sand to westward were suffused with a sunset of tender and delicate brilliance: one of those sunsets that are tranquil and silent, not tumult-uous. And as it deepened the full moon swung slowly up out of the lagoon to the east, a great golden dish with the light running off it like water. It had looked thus one evening long ago, from Anoghia on the flank of Mount Ida: the same full-moon, the same traveller; the reality of freedom, the illusion of captivity. I looked and looked and remembered; and knew that I should never again call up the one scene without the other, and each would be the richer for it.

I had not thought that a landscape could be so near per-fection without mountains; but here palm-grove and sandbank and water were interlaced and reflected, land running into creek and lagoon into land until all seemed ready to cast off and float away into the sky, where grand, isolated clouds raised heads like Ossa and Pelion. It is this extravagance of beauty in life that makes it so intoxicating.

The sunset sank slowly to a glow and went down into the water, which itself took on a shining golden whiteness the colour of new wheat straw. And now a colder, harder light intruded: two great search-lights had been switched on which lit up the causeway from dusk until dawn as a protection against surprise attack. So much the better for me: they gave me once more a rough idea where I must be. I tried to make a guess at how far away they were, but that is difficult with a light unless you have some idea how powerful it is. Still, at the very least they gave me an idea where on the map to look for this crossing.

Such profusion of water-birds I have never seen anywhere in my life. From the little, preoccupied stints and godwits and the like, through egrets to a majestic spoonbill, they were leading their own lives undisturbed and unhurried. I could not get over my luck, to be doing and seeing these things. I thought, Americans would pay a thousand dollars an hour for this, and not see a tenth of what I am seeing, and still they would think themselves a privileged few. And so they would be, if they did see a tenth of it.


At last we reached a curving sandy shore, disembarked (none of them thanked the ferryman; nor had they thanked anyone anywhere else so far as I had seen) and climbed a low, tree- and bush-covered dune. There was a dip on the other side of this, with a sand track running along it, and here our onward transport was waiting for us: a tractor and trailer. But once more the organization's power to organize had fallen short. The tractor had no starter and no crank-handle, and the driver had failed to park it high enough up on the dune to turn the engine over on the run down. Three-quarters of an hour went by while they struggled and pushed and blew upon sparking-plugs and sucked at fuel-pipes. I did not mind. It gave me time to make a detail-map in my head of every contour and clump of trees and angle of track; so that later, on a real map, I was able to recognize the place without the least doubt or trouble. In the end the driver was sent off to a farm in a tuft of palms half a mile away to fetch tools. I added the farm to my mental

63

map; the engine finally thundered into life, and we were off again, PK in glory beside the driver, Tiger Tim and the Third Man and I clinging for dear life to the shallow sides of the trailer.

A strongish night wind had sprung up, and I had been soaking-wet for a good many hours — for most of twenty-four, in fact. Despite the climate I began to get very cold. And then, a tractor is a happily bucolic thing to ride on, whereas being tossed up and down on the trailer is simply a repetitious kind of torture, even when the going is good. Ours was not; we were climbing across causeways and water-courses that looked barely negotiable if at all, and doing it at maximum speed under orders from PK, who was an urban type and probably had little idea what a tractor can do. He was not too uncomfortable himself, whereas we were being tossed like pancakes behind him.

After a good two hours we drew up in the darkness of a big palm-grove. There was a wattle fence with a gate in it; I was led through, and up a path. There was sand underfoot, and I smelt animals. In a hundred yards or so the leaves overhead gave way to a starry circle of sky and I saw that we were in a wide clearing with three or four palm-thatch huts set round it, and little, twinkling oil-wick lights. I was taken to a hut set on slightly higher ground than the others. It must have been about ten feet long by six wide, and consisted of a mud wall like a low parapet, above which straw screens laced on to poles went up to the atap roof on three sides. An oil-lamp standing on the parapet at the open front showed that it was built up on bricks off the ground. A couple of steps went up to a gap in the parapet. Inside was a board floor and against the back wall a raised bed or bench covered with a clean cane mat. *It was clean.* Even now, that is what I remember most distinctly about it. I stumbled across, and almost without knowing it lay down and closed my eyes. I did not want to sleep: I could see that here would be the chance I had been waiting for. But physically I was all-in. After a few minutes I opened my eyes again and looked carefully round. A fire had been lighted near the middle of the clearing, and eight or ten people were moving round it, including PK and the other two. The straw back wall of my hut was loosely fastened: without moving much I pushed it aside a little and looked out into what seemed to be a big wood of palms. No glimmer through the trunks suggested other dwellings, or open country, and the skyline showed leaves receding beyond leaves. Away in front, beyond the track we had come by, I thought I could hear the sea.

I could no more have got up and run than I could have got up and levitated. But, I told myself, if I can just get an hour, say, of rest, then when everything is quiet I shall shove back this screen a little further and slide through the gap, and away into the jungle. After that . . . But 'after that' could take care of itself. The first thing was to get rid of the lamp. I slipped off the bed, blew it out, and returned. Almost before I had lain down again I was asleep or in some state near to it. But not for long. There were voices, a repeated scratching sound: at someone's orders from the fireside a child was re-lighting my lamp. As soon as all backs were turned I blew it out again. Five minutes later the same thing happened. But they had not suspected me; thinking it was the wind, the child put the lamp down on the floor inside the hut, where the parapet sheltered it. It now lit up the interior very much more than before: I should have to wait till it sooted up, or burned low. I slid off into unconsciousness again on the instant.

Someone was gently shaking my foot. A woman stood beside me holding a bowl of steaming food. She set it down carefully, gave a ravishing smile in the light of the lamp, and sank away into the darkness.

The disappointment of being woken made me want to cry like a child.

'Get up and eat,' my internal taskmaster said relentlessly.

65

'You're going to make a run for it in an hour's time: you need fuel.' Still I could not make myself stir; and I thought too that the best thing I could do was to make it clear that I was completely exhausted. They would take the less trouble about staying on the alert. But only a few minutes had passed before PK was standing in front of me. 'You eat now,' he said. 'Five, ten minutes, we go.'

The bottom dropped out of the world for me. It had never entered my head that the night's journey was not over. But there was nothing for it. Impossible to get a mouthful of food down, but I shoved my feet into my sandals again and a comb through my hair, and went to sit on the top step of the hut. The woman came back, looked at me anxiously, carried the food bowl over, patted me, smiled into my face. I think she would have fed me by hand if she had dared. I was touched by her kindness and bewilderment and fear. And, I thought, if I had slipped under the screen and you had seen me go, you wouldn't have told. Yet if you had, I wouldn't have blamed you. There must be children you have to protect.

While I waited for PK and the others to finish eating I looked at this place properly for the first time: that is, for its own sake, not for what chances it might offer. By day perhaps it would have looked mean and dirty, but now by moonlight it was a marvel of beauty. I thought again that the big travel companies would pay fortunes to have access to such a place, straw huts and all; and here was I getting it all for nothing. It seemed a happy irony in these circumstances that I should be being given so grand a tour.

Outside on the track a minibus was waiting and I was told to get in. Exhaustion had closed in on me again and I moved like a zombie, but managed to get a sight of the licence-plate in the glow of the tail-lamp and memorize it. Four armed men got in, but not PK and his henchman; we drove off.

I have no idea how long this next lap of the journey took. The track turned slowly into road but there were few or no lights showing either in the countryside or later, when we were running through streets. It seemed interminable but may have lasted less than half an hour. When we pulled up it was at a steel-shuttered gate which was rolled back disclosing a brightly lighted ramp into a garage, apparently a terrorists' transport park. I could see three or four vehicles; I was ordered down, and memorized the number of the nearest, a big closed van. The minibus was driven in, the gate closed. A dark-coloured saloon car slid alongside us. One of the armed men with me pulled open the back door and bundled me in, another got in on the other side, and we were off again. As soon as we had drawn away the man in the front passenger seat (also armed) turned towards me and said in perfect English without the least trace of accent:

'First of all I must apologise to you for any inconvenience you've been put to in the last few days. Our people down there are only inexperienced boys, and they haven't got the facilities for this sort of thing.'

I was completely taken aback by this language and found myself replying in the same vein, as if to somebody thanking one for some trivial service: not a bit, don't think about it, no trouble at all. 'At any rate,' he said, 'rest assured that from now on we shall make you comfortable. We are sorry that at first conditions were rough; from now on we can offer you something better.' I said I supposed we should go and see Professor N. in the morning, and he agreed. It was gone midnight now, so nothing could be looked for tonight.

I was past thinking anything out, but an uneasiness remained. Instinct was all for accepting that here was a civilized man and a potential helper. But I had had one glimpse, as I got into the car, of his head in silhouette against the lights, and it had been the silhouette of the late Jomo Kenyatta's head, with a pair of steel-rimmed spectacles added. Instinct might be ready to advance as on a dog wagging its tail, but that glimpse had wagged a different message.

We drove through what I recognized from my one earlier visit here as the centre of Jaffna town. As we slowed to come round a steep corner a youth with a rifle jumped out into the road and stopped us. He was probably seventeen, in jeans and a sweatshirt, with crossed ammunition-belts and other fashionable gear. Kenyatta answered his challenge solemnly in Tamil; I heard him say 'EROS' twice, and the boy waved us on. The same thing happened three times more in the course of ten minutes' drive. Then we were clear of the town and running along the top of a steepish slope covered with big coconut palms, the roofs of houses showing between the trunks. We took a turning downhill; there were gates and walls and fences. I got the impression of an expensive seaside suburb for the rich. We turned through a gateway into a short drive between walls, and stopped at a biggish house. The doorway, on our right, faced into the blank concrete shuttering on our left; there was width only for one car. The road and walls ran on past the house, no doubt to another exit. The place was either designed for protection against sudden attack, or chosen because so well suited for it.

Kenyatta led me into a hallway about forty feet long. Trestle tables stood against the back wall, piled with small-arms, mostly AK47s I thought, but I did not risk staring. There was a room on the right with some kind of turmoil going on inside it, and a lot of men were milling about in the hall. Kenyatta unlocked a door on our left and pushed me in. The room was about ten feet square, with a high window, barred on the inside and the glass behind the bars coated with paint. It contained nothing whatsoever except a strip of thin straw mat, filthy dirty, on the still dirtier concrete floor. So I could look forward to comfort from now on?

I thought fast, for I saw that this house was a fortress and once that door shut on me there would be no way out. I stopped and asked primly where I could wash. Kenyatta said something to the nearest of the armed men, who led me through a crowd of others, past two doorways, and thrust me into a big room which not long before had been fitted as an adequate bathroom. It had a channelled tile floor like a stable, a lavatory, broken but still just usable, a hand-basin, broken and unusable, an old oil-drum for refuse, and a length of bent metal pipe which, sagging from the ceiling like a smashed daffodil-stalk, dispensed a trickle of water at the turn of a stopcock. None the less there was ground for hope here. In the far corner was an ill-fitting door secured, as far as I could make out, only by a bolt on the outside. No doubt it was there for the removal and emptying of the oil-drum, so it would be an external door. There was nothing to be seen at present by squinting through the crack, but by daylight there might be.

When I got back across the hall Kenyatta was still waiting, rather impatiently. He pushed me in through the door and I heard the lock turn. I lay down on the straw mat and was asleep in seconds.


In the morning an armed man came in with tea and biscuits and, finding nowhere to put them down, brought a strange-looking metal chair and a kind of miniature stool on which a cup could be set. When he returned to take the cup away I pointed in the direction of the bathroom and he let me go. This time I could see a broad crack down the side of the door, and nearly an inch of the round shaft of a bolt. I searched the room for something I could use to shift it. There was nothing. But, I told myself, don't stop trying, something may turn up. I went back to my room.

Kenyatta arrived, and I asked if we were now going to Professor N. Perhaps, he replied, and began immediately on an interrogation. Like the others, its object appeared to be to trap me into an admission, or at least something my captors could claim was an admission, that I was 'a spy' — meaning that I was employed either by the Sri Lankan government or by a foreign intelligence service. As I was not, it was easy to avoid saying I was; but it is another matter to avoid saying anything that an interrogator can misconstrue. I thanked my stars that I had once been a journalist: it had taught me how to put a sentence together so that its whole sense will not be inverted if a sub-editor should cut it in half.

I could see from their questions that, of all the intelligence organizations they had heard of, the one they feared and hated most was MOSSAD. This was probably a reflection of their Palestinian training in the trade of terrorism. But I saw something else that concerned me more directly. Not only was MOSSAD the organization they hated most, it was the one they most wanted to link me to. It would be the tallest of feathers in their cap, to have caught one of its agents. But there was more than that to it. I realized that they wanted a reason for killing me, not a reason for letting me go. Why should they want that? I could see the answer now and then in their eyes. Power over others was what they thirsted for and rejoiced in above all; and blood is the most thrilling of all proofs of power.


A main difficulty for me was to convince questioners that if not a spy I was equally not a journalist. I had to do this for two reasons. It was true; I had not worked for the Press for thirty years. But – much more important – it was what they would most have liked me to be, failing a spy, for experience had taught them that journalists would generally accept their picture of themselves as 'freedom-fighters'. They were quite open in their approach to this subject. 'You are a journalist. We know. You write nice propaganda for us, we let you go.' It was not difficult to reject these offers of a way out; but I thought that it would be harder if the going got tough. Prudence therefore made me shut the door on myself in advance.

I think my captors found some of this genuinely bewildering. They would naturally have supposed that in my dealings with them my objective was to survive. And in a sense no doubt it was; but the real target upon which my whole effort was concentrated was simply to go honourably through to the end of what I had begun. What the end might turn out to be was of secondary importance.

I said freely that I was a writer, but not of the kind they wanted. Then what did I write? Well, I had written a book of memoirs about Cyprus; and three novels, but none had been published; and occasional articles for magazines, about countries I knew, and a lot of poetry, some being published now. Cross-questioned about the articles, I described them as being about the countries whose entry and exit visas were to be seen in my passport, and hoped to leave the impression that they were about travel. I could hardly say that almost all of them had been about how Communist insurgencies and subversive movements have been, or can be, defeated.

Kenyatta seemed to attach great importance to my possession of a card showing me to be a member of the Royal United Services' Institute. That, he insisted, was proof positive that I worked for MI5. I put it to him that if I did, it would be odd of me to carry a card to say so. I thought he was more than intelligent enough to see that for himself; but he was so anxious to believe in my being an intelligence agent that he went on doing so, and eventually published a statement of it as fact.

Two things became clear the first time that he interrogated me. Every detail of the earlier interrogations had been reported to him; and he was a very different kettle of fish from Ratface and his crew. This man did not belong to the *bandar-log*, he belonged to a much more sophisticated and unpleasant breed. He knew what he was doing. He had a good English education behind him, and whatever his Marxism may have derived from he was no representative of the working class. He was probably not even Tamil, or only partly so. I tried to see somewhere in his eyes or his language a gleam of idealism, but there was nothing there except a steely desire to dominate.

71

I raised the Professor's name again, asking when we were to go there. He said it was difficult now. 'You see, he was expecting you yesterday.' But he did not really bother to make the words sound convincing. I began to see that there had never been any plan to take me to the Professor at all. It had been a trick to keep me co-operating during a journey which the *bandar-log* could hardly have managed if I had not had some inducement to go with them. I felt ashamed of myself for having been so easily fooled. Yet I had half-connived at it, believing in their promises because I wanted to, not because they were believable. I had to weigh the chances of a successful break-and-run against those of wait-and-see, and several times I chose wait-and-see from mixed motives: partly doubt that I could bring off an escape, partly a sense that I had not yet reached the end of the road.

In the doorway Kenyatta turned back and asked if I would like him to telephone Tony for me. I was suspicious, because Ratface had made this offer too and I had been told that it had been done, but then later that it had not. I concluded that it was in the drill-book, perhaps as part of a resistance-lowering technique based on repeatedly raising the prisoner's hopes and then dashing them. (Certainly this was done in a number of ways.) But I wanted so badly to get word to Tony to reassure him that I took the bait, and Kenyatta said he would put the call through himself, straight away. It was still only about 9 o'clock. 'It'll be early in England,' he said with a smile, 'but I don't suppose he'll mind, will he?' He wrote the number down and said he would say I was alive and well and in no serious trouble. Then he added casually, 'Is there any special message you'd like me to pass to him?' He watched my eyes as he asked it, and I saw that I was meant to step into a trap. He had wanted me to give something which he could claim was a coded message, or which actually was one. I said, 'Tell him I love him.' This time I was watching his eyes — and was astonished at what I saw. First was a flash of annoyance that the trap had not been sprung; but displacing that was a real, involuntary smile of human understanding, veiled in its turn by annoyance that the bourgeois concept of marital love should be real after all.

When he had gone I settled down seriously to the question of killing time. The chair was as uncomfortable as the stocks, I ached from head to toe from yesterday's battering on the trailer, and an excruciating din had been going on for an hour or more. When this began I had thought it was some kind of street-procession going past under the window; but although every ten minutes or so it stopped, then began again more softly and climbed to a horrible fortissimo, it never passed. I realized slowly that it was coming out of a record-player in the next room, and that it was some American version of Hindu chanting, apparently directed by a cheerleader with a Middle-Western accent that could have rusted a bulldozer. It was so appalling that it made you laugh, the first few times round; after that it was like having your eardrums sawn in half, and on top of that I was in no mood to listen to my allies being made to sound ridiculous. I cannot believe that it was meant as a form of torture (for one thing, no one in the place was subtle enough for that). Perhaps the *bandar-log* simply liked it.

Among the few possessions in my handbag were a small notepad and a pocket address-book. This had already been the basis for hours of interrogation, and was to generate many hours' more, for all my questioners, Kenyatta included, were sure it contained things which they badly wanted to know. And so it did, and I never ceased blaming myself for having, through pure inefficiency, had it with me. But though they went on and on about this name and that, they never hit on the right ones — that is, those of anyone wealthy or well-known or influential, on whom they might have thought they could put pressure for a bargain, or any writers or offices with a record of anti-terrorist or merely anti-Marxist activity. Such addresses, and those of any members of the Sri Lankan government or armed forces, would have been enough excuse, if recognized, for them to shoot me or do anything else they pleased. I had managed to destroy two or three pages, those likeliest to lead to trouble, and in other places I had simply altered names and telephone numbers. None of these was noticed as suspicious.

I saw that if I was to keep my balance in the conditions I was now in, some kind of occupation was absolutely necessary; and that therefore, since I had nothing to read, I had better write. There was a strong temptation to record every detail about my captors, place of imprisonment, etc., for future use; but obviously if I made such a record it would be taken away from me. That would be worse than doing nothing at all. Either I must learn to live entirely inside my own mind (and I was not ready to do that, yet) or I had better write something I could keep and finish.

I could not start on a novel or a short story: tension closes up those pores through which imagination breathes. But it had been put to me two months earlier that I write some kind of memoirs. I had thought it a pointless and bad idea at the time, and though I had made a start I had put it aside. Now it seemed I could do worse than go on. I should have to keep only to such times and incidents as could give my captors no clue at all about me or my family; where they could be reached, whether they could raise ransoms, who they might be, what I had ever done. Nor must I leave gaps that might encourage guessing, for that would fuel the interrogators, and again, the book would be taken away from me. But luckily there was an almost self-contained phase of my life that fell well within these limitations, and better still, it was a phase especially suitable for thinking about, now. For it was my first taste of total freedom.

In 1951 I had gone to Greece alone, in the teeth of heavy

74

opposition from my family. At that time the civil war was not long over; the country was very near starvation and some districts were still under arms. There were no tourists, and few or no facilities for them outside Athens. Before the war my family might have had friends or contacts there, and it would have seemed natural to their generation to ask these to keep an eye on me; but at this time they knew no one who could be unofficially relied on. True, a friend had written to a friend, the US Consul-General, and asked him to book a room for me in some suitable place: but this link might or might not amount to anything. (In the event, he and his wife were endlessly kind to me and we became great friends. I still feel grateful to them.) But to my parents and their kind, girls simply did not travel alone. A girl alone would inevitably get into difficulties; would have to be helped by some stranger who might take advantage of her ignorance and could hardly be blamed if he did, for to risk such things is tantamount to asking for them. To my parents this was as plain as that two and two make four.

It was not plain to me at all, but I knew nothing of the risks they had in mind. I was no fledgling when I first set out. I had lived and worked among strangers in wartime London and I thought myself not entirely green. But, because the walls of decency and civilization had not collapsed along with the blackened brickwork, I remained more innocent and ignorant of the animal underside of human nature than any child is today. Things which are now shown daily on domestic TV screens I had not only never heard of: if anyone had tried to tell me of them I should have dismissed them as fantasies of a diseased mind.

Being now a prisoner, with a prisoner's routine problems to solve, it seemed to me that nothing in my life had prepared me half so well for the present phase of it as travelling on foot about Greece; for I had begun then to learn to ignore exhaustion and not to be cast down by rough conditions and rougher going. I had been acting then of my own free will, not with a gun close to my head, but the difference was not so great as I might have supposed. I knew already that the beauty of that crossing of the lagoon, for instance, would stay with me for the rest of my life.

So, a lot older now and it may be thought not much wiser, I decided the time was at last ripe for remembering the first flights of a tyro bumble bee. I began to write, as small as I could, using first the scribbling-pad and the odd scraps of paper in my handbag, then the unfilled pages in the address-book, and eventually writing upside-down between filled lines, and carrying on roughly from where I thought I had left off. What follows is the result.

I could afford only two days in Delphi, but the pull was too strong — not of Delphi only but of Parnassus itself. There is a grand, golden, ancient detachment about Parnassus, as if it were truly our first home. I cut down eating to a minimum and stayed on. The owner of the Little House saw me counting my dwindling drachmas. He made a speech with gestures conveying the expense of eating out; then taking me by the hand he led me down into the cave-like dwelling below the balcony where his family lived, and invited me to share their midday meal. Kinder or more courteous hosts I could not have had. The room, though very dark, was very clean. We ate tomatoes and potatoes cut up and sprinkled with oil and herbs, little hard black olives, and huge chunks of dark bread. They showed me how to break off pieces and plunge them in the oil before eating then. I found it difficult to do at first.

The next morning I developed a brief but violent feverish cold which left me two days later feeling weak in the limbs and head (the last no uncommon state with me, I am told). I set out to walk across a valley-head towards a monastery whose dome I had seen, sky-blue against olive-blue and pine-green, four or five miles away, I guessed. I knew nothing as yet of the tricks that Greek light plays with distance.

After three hours the dome seemed to have got no nearer, though it had appeared and disappeared many times, like a conjuror's egg. I forget how long I went on before it occurred to me that I had better give up for the day and turn back towards Delphi while the light lasted, otherwise I should have not the least idea which way to go. Blaming myself for incompetence and lack of determination, I plodded along goat-paths and mule-tracks, over spurs, down glimmering gullies and up again out of them, while legs and head got weaker and I had not the sense to think why. At last I felt that I was not going to get very much further. But I came round a corner, and there in the middle of the track, glowing and smooth and lightly filmed with dust, lay a huge ripe tomato, rolled there out of some mule's pannier. I stopped and looked at it, and looked at it. Probably it was no more than forty-eight hours since I had eaten; but an idea now formed itself quite clearly in my mind. Either I dust off this tomato which the patron saint of fools has sent me, and eat it, and go on until I reach Delphi; or I don't, and I don't get back to Delphi either. I had never in my life picked something up off a road and eaten it, but there is a first time for everything – and even such trivial first times as this have a knack of staying in the memory. I ate the tomato, sitting with my feet dangling over a valley bloomed with dusk, and when I got up again the fog had cleared from my eyes and mind and my legs were serviceable once more.

It was long after dark when I got back to the Little House, but I felt elated and invincible (a dangerous illusion which I have often suffered from since). I had proved myself to be on the contrary hopelessly easily vincible. But I had also learned the first of many elementary lessons about travel. Food is necessary.

I am using that word 'travel' to mean going in order to find things out, for their own sakes, not for some purpose unrelated to the journey; and for pleasure in that journey itself, for escaping from imagination into reality, not for mere sight-seeing. An objective to be reached or fulfilled concentrates the thoughts and sharpens enthusiasm; and it adds body to the enjoyment, too, like the biscuits in a charlotte. But it should not be one that will put a constraint on time, or the juice of the journey will get squeezed out by the logistics. More chances are lost by pushing on in order to reach a given place at a fixed time, than in any other way.

I had, as you might say, cut my teeth on Delphi. Back in Athens a new friend (who became a lifelong one) roughed out an itinerary for me to follow by local buses and on foot; he estimated that it would take up most of the remaining fortnight that my funds could stand. (The fortnight became a year and a half, but that could not have been foreseen.) I set out at 5 o'clock one brilliant August morning for the bus terminal in Chateaubriand Street, much like Dick Whittington but without the cat. Some hours later the bus put me down at Diakofto, half-way along the northern shore of the Peloponnese. This is the starting-point for a unique rack-and-pinion railway, designed and built in 1881 by the French engineer and novelist Edmond About. Despite their formidable talent for destruction the Greeks had kept the train exactly as About had built it, tall flared funnel, brass fittings, panelled and varnished carriages, lamps, steam-whistles and all. This amazing construction climbs straight up the mountain side for about 800 feet, crossing spectacular gorges, and comes to a standstill at last in a pomegranate bush close to the Megaspileion – a great complex of caves once filled with monasteries, tragically destroyed by fire during the German retreat through Greece.

When I had got clear of the pomegranate bush I struck off across the hill roughly in the direction suggested by my map – a pretty-coloured affair from a paper-shop, which later turned out to be a work of beguiling fiction.

People who walk, or do anything more active, generally

seem to want to know about each other's kit, down to the dullest details, so let me say now that my knapsack contained a change of underclothes and shirt, a pair of very lightweight, dark-coloured silk pyjamas (worth their negligible weight in gold), a towel, washing-kit, comb, talcum (against blisters), sticking-plaster, paper and pencil, piece of string, two yards of parachute-cord (because I happened to have it, and it looked handy), pocket-knife (Whittington would never have got to London without a pocket-knife); small plastic box containing cheese, bread, and olives, and a small tin flask of water; a phrase-book, a pocket modern Greek grammar, and a pocket lexicon. I wore a cotton shirt and skirt (trousers on a girl would have been thought indecent in the Greek countryside at that time, and they are not much liked by older people, even now); very strong sandals (as supplied to the monks of Buckfast Abbey, the salesman had told me); and on John Leatham's advice I carried a large woollen jersey, an infernal nuisance by day but necessary at night for I did not possess a sleeping-bag. In those days they were expensive luxuries.

The phrase-book was not much help, being too tied up in 'When will my washing be ready?' or 'Does the train leave from this platform?' — stuff that was not much more useful on a walk than the little I could remember from an early attempt to learn ancient Greek under the bedclothes after hours. ('Neither poets nor sailors ride well.' Oh, well . . . 'Even the police now want to dance in the streets.') But the grammar and the dictionary were worth rubies. I had also prepared myself before setting out with nine words, carefully chosen and carried as it were at the ready, for rapid fire when a target was identified. They were *Please* and *Thank you*, *Yes* and *No*, *Left* and *Right*, *Bread*, *Wine* and *Water*. It seemed to my ignorance that these would be a good basis for coping with likely emergencies.

I soon found that only two of them were necessary, and four could be counter-productive. *Please* and *Thank you* were needed at every brush with humanity, and must be so in every country in the world. But *Yes* and *No* could boomerang, for *Yes* in Greek is *Nai*, and when I wanted either in a hurry, the wrong one was likely to emerge first. *Left* and *Right* confuse the average shepherd, for he is only at home with north. He looks down at his hands, and then speaks very determinedly, and you finally go on your way not knowing whether he meant left as you were standing or as he was. As for bread, wine and water, where they were to hand they would all be given to you before you could reasonably ask for them.

I hoped that *Left* and *Right* might at least come in useful when I got back to Athens, but they hardly did. As a Greek friend explained to me, it is no use asking a woman the way, she generally doesn't know or can't explain. So you must ask a man, and if he knows where you want to go, he will take you there. If he only tells you, it's because he doesn't know.

I have sometimes thought since about what a basic word-list for beginners in a strange country should include. Obviously something of the nature of 'It's very good'; otherwise you will often seem churlish. *Who* and *When* must come near the top; and the Greeks' own front-running question is *Why?* — which may account for much of their history. *Come* and *Go* are valuable, but not necessary because they can be mimed. For myself, two of the most essential phrases are 'It doesn't matter' and 'I'm *so* sorry'. But that is all a matter of how inept you are. Strangers are incredibly kind; misunderstanding something you have said or done, they will go to inordinate lengths to get you a claw-hammer or a photograph of the late Queen Amalia in the belief that that is what you want. A quick 'It doesn't matter' may sometimes stop this problem getting out of hand. But your own misprisions will range much wider and more damagingly. The whole field of confusion and error is open. So when you have provoked dismay or outraged local feeling unwittingly, there is nothing you can do but say 'I'm *so* sorry', and mean it; and try to find out afterwards what your mistake was.

As you advance in a language a need develops for phrases to extricate yourself from hospitality and attention. ('You will

80

come to my village' ... 'stay in my house' ... 'attend my daughter's wedding', and so on.) I came back from my first trip knowing that a milestone in learning a language is the ability to say: 'I would have loved to have done it (gone there, come back next week, etc.), but...' I had never before glimpsed the importance of subjunctives. These are the real-life uses of grammar, and if only children were told so the subject might appeal to them more.

My first day wore on, the hills unrolled before and behind me, and I became filled as a pitcher is filled from a spring with such a sense of freedom as I had scarcely dreamed of. The solitude had as much to do with it, I think, as the space. We may be group animals by nature, but it is our fellow men who circumscribe our freedom — which is ironic, since so much of the freedom we possess is gained only by dint of men gathering together.

I sat under a stunted thorn tree on a stony hillside, and ate, and was as happy as I had ever been in my life. As I walked on, and as the sun grew nearer to the hills than to the zenith, I began to consider where I should spend the night. It had been explained to me over a lunch in the House of Commons that in Greece all bona fide travellers, regardless of sex, customarily put up in monasteries, and this I intended to do if I could come to one at the right time of day. According to my map a large village called Lampeia lay a few miles ahead. For all I knew there might be a monastery near it. On the other hand I had never tried to follow a map course by sun and guesswork: Lampeia might easily not be ahead of me at all. I half-hoped it wasn't. It seemed to me that it would be immensely strange and delightful to lie down in the shelter of a rock on an empty hillside and go to sleep like a partridge. This may sound ridiculous today, when millions do the same each year on all the hills accessible off charter-flights. There is no longer room to wonder 'What is this going to be like?' The risk is that it may turn out to be a little like a night in an airport transit-lounge. But in those days it was another matter. I had never slept out alone in a lonely place; perhaps I did not even know anybody who ever had, except on service in wartime. I therefore did not know what it would be like, and excitement resides in not knowing. Russian roulette would not be exciting if you knew which chamber was loaded. But nothing is really wearisome as long as you do not know how it may come out. (For that reason I am not finding captivity really wearisome, today.)

Most people I knew would have thought it highly dangerous to sleep out on a Greek mountainside. ('*Anything* might happen.') I knew quite well that this was nonsense. There are no wolves and very few snakes in the Peloponnese. A shepherd there might be, moving his flock overnight to a new pasture; I thought I would keep an ear open, during my last hour of walking, and if I heard a dog barking or the tonk of a bell I would go on a bit further, avoiding being seen, before I settled. Not that I envisaged rape and villainy, or anything of that kind. The little I knew of shepherds suggested that they are not like that at all. But I should have been constrained by the presence of a stranger, and it might have been difficult to get him to go away and let one settle down: he would want to try and talk, and view the odd phenomenon of a foreigner here, and would probably try and make me go with him, out of hospitable concern for my well-being.

The reality was that I was falling in love with solitude. I wanted to have the stars to look at all night long and to be alone with them, and to find out whether I could sleep without bed or shelter, whether I could reduce my wants to what nature supplies. I suppose this urge is in most of us, and that is why Robinson Crusoe tales have such a wide appeal.


Well before sundown I came on a good track, and following it round the shoulder of a hill saw below me a valley full of vines and walnut trees, and a girl and a young man picking the walnuts. They saw me and waved and I waved back; they came bounding up the hill and sprang on to the track beside me. I think I was the first foreigner they had ever met, and we walked down into the village together, eating walnuts: green and juicy, the kernels coiled like ears and as sweet and white as milk. The girl, Angeliki, had a few words of English, to my great surprise, and with the aid of the dictionary we managed to exchange a few basic facts about ourselves. What we said I have forgotten, but the word for walnuts has never left me again, though it is not the most useful you could have. It reminds me of her to this day.

There were eight or ten houses in the village, and one was a taverna, where they made me sit down. Water was brought, and *loukoumi* powdery with sugar; and the girl went to fetch her father. He was a small, lean man, as hard and dark as a branch of olive-wood, dressed in black, with sharp, bright eyes like a rook's. He had spent five years in the United States when he was young, and still remembered a fair bit of English (hence Angeliki's smattering). What American accent he had picked up was not in the least like the strident nasality of today. No doubt speech and voices change more than we think in fifty years.

He laid it down as something not for argument that I should stay in his house. I tried, out of embarrassment or shyness, to say that I meant to walk on for an hour or two more, but I was overborne from all sides. Anyway, they asked, where would I walk on to? There was not another village in thirty miles. I began to feel rather crestfallen about my map-reading. Could it be as bad as that? I said I had been aiming for Lampeia. Was it far away, and in which direction? There's no such place, all their faces said, and the old man said it in words. I showed it to them on the map, but they shook their heads to warn against trusting in things put together on paper in offices by ignoramuses. The man who made the map could never have been here. Everyone would have seen him if he had.

Where are we now? I asked, hoping to get some clue. Prioni,

they said. It was not marked, and all shook their heads again, gloomily delighted with this confirmation of their views.

Later I learned that Lampeia was the district in which Prioni lay, but the name was not used for a village at all.

We talked for at least an hour — and I found that I was learning faster than I had thought possible, looking up words, stringing them together and spouting them, to produce loud delight and grave corrections from the old man. At last (later I realized that he had been delaying to give his wife time to prepare a meal) he got up and led me to his house: the best in the village. Building-stone had been dug out of the hillside, leaving a quarry-face about ten feet high near the track. The house was built up from the bottom of the quarry, its nearest wall some six feet out from the cliff; but its lower floor was used only as a stable. Up on the level of the track the house itself stood clear, a neat square stone construction carrying the stable walls upwards and capped with a red tile roof. There were two windows on this side, shuttered, with pots of basil standing on the sills; and a handsome panelled wood door with a brass knocker. The only way of reaching it was across a kind of drawbridge of two wobbly seven-inch planks spanning the six-foot gap.

The inside was all one large room — perhaps twenty feet by sixteen. Near the door was a free-standing circular hearth of whitewashed bricks, and approximately above it a galvanized pipe was set in a hole in the roof. Against the wall leaned or hung various cooking utensils, all very large to my eyes: milk pans, a kneading trough, a macaroni board, and the like. At the far side in one corner was a large bed piled with sheepskins. Along the wall beyond its foot were ranged three Victorian wagon-topped trunks. Precariously on the centre one, which was spread with a white embroidered cloth, stood a lamp under an icon on a stone projecting from the wall; and on a metal bracket secured to the wall nearby stood a 1930s radio (wireless, I should say), though there was no electricity within thirty miles or more. It too was spread with a white embroidered cloth. It was a caste-mark, a visible proof of social position.

In the end wall of the room was the sort of doorway found in barns, through which grain-sacks hoisted up by rope and pulley can be swung in. On the left of the door was a small bed, and finally in the middle of the room stood a very small wooden table and three rush-bottomed, battered chairs. That seemed to be the total of the family's possessions. True, the trunks would hold a certain amount (one would contain Angeliki's dowry); but it did not seem much, for what was obviously rated locally as a wealthy family. I thought that the trunks would have been of more use if they had had flat tops. But later I was to see many more of them; they are traditional as dowry-chests and I have never seen a flat-topped one yet. I cannot think that there were ever enough Victorian travellers in Greece to account for the number of round-topped trunks still extant, even allowing for the awesome quantities of luggage that such people had. The lives of artefacts have some limit. I fear that somewhere there is a factory still turning them out.

A fourth chair was borrowed; we dined on beans and *feta* cheese; when dusk fell Angeliki put on her good dress and called her cousin Toula, and we went out together to join the *volta*. Greek social life outside the main cities has been nil for many centuries; the custom of the *volta* fills the gap. As anywhere else in the Mediterranean, the girls parade up and down the village street in giggling groups, or sedately with their parents, and the young men do the same but in the opposite direction. Thus they can look each other over (all have got themselves up to the nines), and meet as if by accident as they pass and repass. The *volta* in Prioni did not add up to a throng, but it was not the less important and appreciated for that.

Angeliki was a strong, good-looking girl, fair-complexioned for a Greek peasant, with the wide-set eyes of ancient statues, as grey as Athena's, but perhaps with a touch too much character showing in them to promise perfect married bliss. Toula was a little dark flashing beauty. But it was Angeliki who had the suitors. There was a lightly built, lively young man, full of laughter, clearly the catch of the village; Toula confided to me that his family had asked hers to negotiate for Angeliki. But there was weakness in his face. He would not make a good husband for long, and perhaps not a good provider either. Angeliki asked me to compare him with the young man who had been picking the walnuts with her — and who also came to join us in the *volta*. He had reddish fair hair; he looked strong and sensible rather than handsome. I thought that they were in love and that they would be well matched: it would be a pity if the village Lothario were to carry off the prize. But it transpired that red-hair was her cousin (of course: otherwise it would not have been proper for her to be alone with him in the walnut valley). In the Orthodox Church cousins are within the forbidden degrees of kinship — as are godchildren of the same godparent. In remote places this restriction can bear so hard on the young that godparents will sponsor children of only one sex. I felt sad for Angeliki and her cousin. The wealthy can sometimes flout the Church's restrictions, but there was no hope for these two, and there was something strongly sympathetic about them both.

When we got back to the house an oil-wick was lighted, rugs and hand-embroidered sheets were dragged out of one of the trunks, and a bed was made up on the floor. I bid against Angeliki for the use of this, but the old man issued orders and that was that. Then he said gruffly: 'You want to change your clothes: I look this way.' And he turned on his elbow to the wall. I gratefully and hurriedly climbed into my pyjamas (the others had simply taken off some of the top layer), and the light was blown out.


The next day began by starlight. We dressed and tidied up beds. Last night's dishes had been put outside on to a kind of platform built out at the uphill end of the house: an open-air kitchen. The ashes of the fire were swept together, but no water was put on to heat. The old man went out; the old woman beckoned to me to follow her and crossing the planks led me up a slippery little path past some chickens and a patch of beans. It was still dark, but against the sky in front of me I made out a round roof of thatch supported not on walls but on a ring of stakes about two feet high. A pig-sty. The old lady signed to me to squeeze between the stakes, and she retreated. So did the pig, with grunting courtesy. When I got back Angeliki showed me how to stand on the planks and wash from a minuscule tap let into a gallon petrol-tin hanging on the wall beside the door (filled with water, not petrol). She held the soap, towel and comb, and handed them to me as I needed them. (In Turkey, as I learned later on, these services are often carried further. The water is brought in a curly-spouted tin jug and it can be difficult to prevent the daughter of the house from washing you herself, as she would a baby.)

The old man returned and stumped into the house saying to me 'Come,' and he set on the table what he had been down into the village to fetch. It was a glass of neat ouzo. 'Breakfast,' he said in the confident tone of one who knows foreign ways and enjoys being a good host; and I realized with dismay that he meant it not for himself but for me. I tried to make him drink it instead, but I might as well have been talking to the mountain. In the end, under his eyes, I downed it, and hoping for the best went out to the stable with Angeliki to help put a wooden saddle on the donkey and load it up with buckets, fodder and other things. The old man came and took the mule out. Angeliki and I set off with the donkey by a different way, across a spur of the mountain.

I had no idea what was coming next, and Angeliki did not manage to tell me — not so much for lack of language as because she supposed that normal daily life would be the same to anyone. In half an hour or less we came out from the rocky arms of the hills on to a little flat smooth pasture, perhaps half a mile across; it was dotted here and there with shade-trees, sparkling in the first warm brilliance of the sun, and patched with flocks of grazing sheep and a few very small cows. Below a poplar tree was a well, where a mule walked slowly round and round, turning the pole that turned the screw that raised the buckets. Herdsmen went to and fro fetching water, and under the trees were little groups of young men and girls desultorily watching their flocks, picking flowers, competing with each other at high-jumps, long-jumps, pitching at the mark, sprints, making daisy-chains, and outdoing each other in song. It was the life described by Theocritus, 2000 years out of its time, being lived as naturally as other people lead lives of tractor-driving or catching a bus to an office.

In this eclogue we remained, putting down fodder for draught animals, carrying water, shifting pickets, giving and taking the flowers, admiring the songs, until gone eleven, when the fierceness of the sun took the fun out of life for both men and beasts. Then Angeliki's uncle, who shepherded her father's flock, took them off down the hill; we hung the empty buckets on the donkey again and made our way back to the house, where a meal was waiting for us of goat's cheese, tomatoes swimming in olive oil, and dark, strong, delicious cartwheel bread.

By now I had got over any difficulties about eating bread dipped in oil. The secret is to add plenty of the coarse salt which is always there — and which you need anyway by the time you get to table. Later you progress to eating bread and oil with cloves of garlic too; though I confess I never got to eating the garlic on its own, as some say they do.

The house was spotlessly clean. Everything that could be whitewashed was whitewashed: everything was in its exact place; bread trough and macaroni board were scoured till the wood was silver. The floor was swept after every operation with a corn-straw broom, and the dust was carefully brought together and pushed through two knot-holes in the boards on to the backs of the animals below.

At this first morning meal with the Spanos family I learned another most useful lesson. The Greek peasant, who works as hard as anyone on earth and keeps healthy to a good old age, does it without so much as a mouthful crossing his teeth until he knocks off near midday. From then on I have never been a slave to breakfast; I eat and enjoy it if it is there, but I have never again been bothered if it is not. Another inch gained in the long climb to freedom from trivia.

When I had eaten I took up my knapsack and said I must go. They said I must not. What was the point, anyway? There was a road not far away, and presently a car would come along it. (The word they used means a cart, but since the coming of the internal combustion engine it has served for anything from a village bus to a Mercedes.) The car would not come today; probably not tomorrow; but one day quite soon. Why not wait for it? To bolster the argument, the old man began telling me things that he reckoned must interest me. He told me that it was vitally important to keep the English in Greece, as the Bulgarians would invade if ever they saw the chance, and rape every man, woman and child in the country. (He had not quite the vocabulary to say this, but sprang about making his meaning clear in dumb-show.) He told me that he had fifty gold sovereigns under the bed, for Angeliki's dowry. (These were of course some of the gold sovereigns brought in by the British officers who fought with the Greek Resistance, to pay their way with. By now the coins had become the basic currency of the country, at a rate well above their specie value. They were not coinage: they were as you might say facsimile medals or tokens, and as they were not the legal tender of any country they could be used lawfully in barter. A year or two later an Italian firm hit on the idea of minting great quantities of them and putting them on sale in Greece. But although they were the same as the original British ones, and contained exactly the same amount of gold, the Greeks did not want them for the sole reason that they were Italian. Almost everyone learned how to recognize them, and refused to pay more than about half the proper rate for them; the Italians eventually went home with a gold flea in their ears.)

I stayed in Prioni for another day, or it may even have been longer. I had been becalmed and had lost hold on reality — which happens easily when you are learning fast, because time loses significance. Also I had discovered where I was. Since the age of fourteen or so two lines from the *Greek Anthology* had run in my head: 'Dolphins shall feed in the forests of Erymanthus, and fleet deer in the grey sea.' And now I was on the flank of Erymanthus. The wild improbabilities of life's coincidences are enough to unhinge the sanest.

I left on foot again, intending to make for a crossroads where the bus, if it were coming, would overtake me and carry me to the village I wanted. This too was not called by the name on my map; it was called Divry. In Prioni they had identified it by its position on a road and a river. It had never been called by the map name, they said, but some demarch out to aggrandize himself (this was easily shown by gestures) had had something built, and had then renamed the whole place in his own honour. The map-makers would have got it from the demarchy office.

Before I left I had tried to pay for my board and lodging, and met an indignant refusal. The women simply tilted their heads and backed away. The old man's face darkened with anger and he thundered out: 'No money passes in this house!' There was no way round this. In the end I took their names and addresses from them, wrote to them from Athens, and at Christmas sent presents of things bought for them in England (to avoid the risk of hurting pride): English woollen socks for the patriarch, black wool stockings for the old lady, and a scarlet scarf for Angeliki.

Country women at this time dressed to a very rigid code. The older ones all, without exception, wore black bodices with high necks and long sleeves, full black skirts down to their ankles, and black headscarves which they arranged on their heads in a distinctly noble, Demeter-like way, not the least like black-mammy or Mrs Mop. Girls were allowed as much finery as their parents could afford or would approve – not much, as a rule, and with emphasis on modest covering up; and as brides they were allowed to continue with it for the first few months. But as soon as they started to show their first child they went into the same kit as their mothers. If their husbands could and would afford it, they were allowed russet instead of black – the colour that in Scotland is called moorit or murrey. But from the day of the first death in the family they went into black and never came out of it again. If they did not marry they made the same transition anyway, only a little later. Thus the days of girlish glory were short, much time and trouble were saved, and money was put by for the real economic burden: the provision of dowries for sisters and daughters.

Marriage without a dowry was almost out of the question, and the amount affected both family honour and the treatment the bride could expect from her mother-in-law. All the men in a family had to contribute to the dowries, and the girls themselves started work on their chest of household linen and clothes from the day they could hold a needle. A custom widely held to forbade young men to marry until all their sisters had been found husbands. This caused great suffering, and probably more hardship than good to the girls themselves. For it left them little hope of saying no to a truly detested match; and while the brothers in one family were kept in enforced bachelordom the sisters in another must whistle for husbands. The system served less to help in getting girls married than in keeping down the population.


One of the most useful things I discovered in this first long walk was that the language problem – though of course it remained – was not a serious block to what I wanted to do. I had only a handful of words as yet; but the dictionary was always there and the grammar-book had given me some slight notion of how verbs were used. At need I could make myself understood. I had found too that it was worth while to think of the long word in English for what I wanted. Probably it had an ancient Greek derivation; then a little playing about with modern pronunciation rules, and someone — usually a schoolchild — would say: 'She means such-and-such.' I provoked fountains of mirth when I tried to say things, but that was only right and fair. Strangers often put themselves to great trouble for me: how could I grudge them an innocent laugh in return?

There was no bus, and I was glad; I took another look at my map and walked on. The monastery sandals were superb: my feet, which had never been treated like this before, gave no trouble worth noticing. But Divry was a long way off, and by the time it came in sight at last I was hardly moving in first gear. I knew that there was in it a Hotel of Sleep. At the time these were few and far between, and they were reputed to be often little better than brothels. The proper thing for decent women therefore was to go to a convent or monastery or any private house, unless she had reliable guarantees that a specific hotel was all right. This was the case with the Divry Hotel of Sleep; someone in Prioni was related to the owner, knew that it was respectable, that it would be all right to go there; he had given me a note for the owner's wife to say that I must be looked after. The outside of the place did not inspire, but I was past carping. As I went up the steps I felt thankful that it was at the near end of the main street.

Unusually it had a restaurant attached to it, occupying the ground floor. My note caused stir and anxiety, for the hotel was full. What could be done? (The owner had a smattering of English, so I was kept abreast of what was going on.) Perhaps I needed a meal? Whilst I was eating they would see what they could arrange for me. I fell on to a chair, rather than sat down on it, and ordered a plate of macaroni with meat sauce. I was ravenous. When it came it looked a little like the inner pipes of something, but it smelled marvellous. I took a mouthful, and it tasted marvellous. I took another, and found I could hardly get it down. The stuff still seemed just as good, but my stomach was too tired to start work. I could not understand this. I had heard that one could be too tired to want to eat, but surely not literally too tired to be able to, so long as one was awake? And what about the earlier lesson with the tomato? But it was no good. I waited, and tried again, but if I had had to force another mouthful down I should have returned it.

At last I was saved by the arrival of the proprietress. A room had been found for me, only there was no bed. One was being fetched out of the next house. A few minutes later it was carried through the dining-room and up the stairs, watched by curious diners; and at last, almost caved-in, I was led upstairs after it.

The room already contained two beds, one occupied by a young girl and one by a woman, both of them asleep despite the racket. I was astonished. It had never occurred to me that a hotel, however lowly, would pack strangers into its rooms like rabbits into a hutch. Today you may take a room for £150 in a five-star hotel in a Gulf State, and come back after dinner to find it full of interlopers with their eyes shut. But in 1951 in Western Europe such things did not happen – or not to my knowledge. Still, I told myself, it's a lot better than standing in the street. And it was not three minutes before I was in the third bed and the light out and I with it. There was an enormous hole in the springs and the mattress was already sinking through it, and so was I before long. I remember pulling myself out once, having reached the floor; and the light coming on again later, and people trying to lug yet a fourth bed in, and asking me to move mine. I seem to remember wanting to say, 'Enough's enough; and if anyone touches this wire toast-rack it'll collapse, and you can take it out and I'll get into this

93

new one' — and then thinking, 'Some miserable woman is standing out there wondering where to lay her head, as I was an hour or two ago.' But which thought prevailed I do not know. Probably I never got as far as saying anything before I was asleep again.

The next day the daughter of the Hotel of Sleep walked me round to see the sights, and showed me a new reservoir which had been the cause of the demarchal swollen head and the renaming of the village. She was a charming girl with big eyes and careful, very precise English learned from the radio. Her only difficulty was with words starting on a *d*. She spoke repeatedly of a honkey, and I thought it a great improvement.

Somewhere between Divry and Olympia the bus stopped for refuelling. As we sat waiting for it a hangdog sort of man of unusual ugliness came by, pulling behind him a sullen mule and a cart. People in the street pointed after him and laughed, saying that he was a thief. They clearly thought it extraordinary, and a very ridiculous thing to be, bound to astonish any stranger.

These roadside stops presented problems, for a foreigner was treated like a guest. If you looked sleepy or determined to be alone, you would be left in peace; but when you tried to pay your bill you would find that someone had already paid it. If you were not obviously anxious for silence, one person at a time would come and talk to you. Others would sit a little way off and wait their chance, but not stare meantime, and children would be shooed away. A Homeric pattern of good manners was still traceable in the way conversations were then developed. News of the day would be exchanged but no personal questions asked until water and *loukoumi*, or water and coffee, or wine and *mezedakia*, had been brought and you had restored yourself with them. Even then the first steps would be formal: Whence comest? Whither goest? From what country? and so on. Immense importance was attached to country. Few Greeks outside cities had seen enough foreigners to be sure of telling English from German; whilst in their minds the English were St George and Germans were the foul dragon.

94

True, there were very few Germans in Greece then, but black memories of them were still fresh, and those who did come seemed amazingly insensitive to the scorn and hatred that their nation had inspired. But among Greek good qualities is a fine talent for mentally separating the individual from his kind, so that any one German was likely to be sized up on his own apparent merits at that moment. Still, it was impossible to miss the change in faces if anyone asked, 'Are you German?' and got the answer: 'No, English.' (It seemed always to be taken for granted that the question would be answered truthfully, and I more than once saw Germans take advantage of this.)

Between Divry and Olympia I first saw the custom, when giving someone a glass of water, of pouring a little of it on to the ground. Different reasons for this are cited. It is to rinse the rim of the glass before you put it to your mouth; to commemorate Christ's baptism; to pour off the dust that might have gathered on the surface on the way; to signify the water that ran when Christ's side was pierced by the spear; and so on. But though no one ever says so I am sure that it descends directly from the ancient Greek custom of pouring a libation to the Earth Mother. Originally it would have been of milk, but later of other things. Various Christian or hygienic ideas have been attached to the action in due time, and that is surely all.

Once in a taverna where I had praised the wine, the proprietor replied that I had not tasted his best: it was never served at the tables. But would I come down to the cellar and try it?

The cellar was cold and dark, clay-floored, smelling of earth and must, with very low brick arches, like eyebrows, tight up under the joists, and a line of huge tuns almost touching them. He took a lamp and the usual little tin cup, and began drawing off swigs from this barrel and that, for he said I must compare one with another. By the time we reached his best I was not feeling so finely critical, perhaps, and he, who had been well ahead of me before the tasting started, was walking rather curiously on his heels. But the wine was all that he had said of it, so I was distressed, after he had moved me on to yet another comparison, to look back and see that he had left the spigot-tap open. I drew his attention to it, not without difficulty. When he had got it in focus his face puckered with dismay. Then it cleared; he flung his arm outwards and downwards, palm open, towards the floor. 'Is not the Earth our mother?' he asked. 'And shall we drink, and she go thirsty?' And he turned and strode unsteadily on.

Kenyatta had a lot more questions to ask, mainly aimed to uncover some sinister reason why I had been at Mullaitivu. It seems that natural bullies — that breed which our generation has succumbed to, be they Nazis or Communists, Tamils or Argentines — all share a self-defeating weakness: they want the answer they want, not the true one. So they end up by telling their victims more than they learn from them, and having to make up for themselves most of what they may report to their masters.

On the second day the Professor was not even mentioned. I asked Kenyatta if he had telephoned to Tony, but he said roughly, 'I couldn't get through,' and this time I knew he was lying. He had neither tried to get through nor meant to. So much the better, I thought; if you had brought me word from him I should have found it hard to see you as an enemy.

After dark he arrived carrying a plastic shopping-bag, and said we were off to a new and better place. I thought: with luck it can't be much worse. We drove for about twenty minutes through the suburbs of Jaffna, but the night was overcast and I could not tell even roughly what direction we were going in. When we stopped it was at a house much like the previous ones: that is, it was large, brand-new or not yet finished, and stood in its own well-fenced garden. Like the last one, its main door was at right angles to a narrow approach-road, and with a blast-wall facing it.

But this time Kenyatta had been telling the truth: it was a better place. I was put into a comparatively clean room containing a plank bed with a thin cover and a miniature, rock-hard bolster, a metal chair, and a table, cracked and encrusted with dirt but large and solid. No one who has not been a prisoner can have any idea what a luxury a table is. There was also a small, highly coloured but unappealing picture of a Hindu goddess in one corner, with a minute bracket-shelf under it, and a large, locked wooden cupboard. I never learned what this contained, though I found out, by trying to shift it, that its contents were very heavy. Once two men came to open it up, but I was taken out of the room while they did so and not given a chance to see what they took away.

The window, like the others, had frosted glass and a strong iron grille on the inside. The sanitary arrangements at the far end of the building were marginally better than in the last house, but only marginally, and there was no possibility whatever of a break-out from them. (That first impression was confirmed from many thorough examinations later.) Kenyatta glanced over them himself; I think he had expected to show me something suitable to the image of modernity that he had been trying to build up, and a look of exasperation crossed his face. It was almost as if he had said aloud: 'You give these people a new, decent place to live in, and it takes them a week to reduce it to the level of a jungle hut.'

We went back to my room and he threw his shopping-bag on the bed. 'These are for you,' he said. The bag contained a towel, a hand-towel, two rolls of lavatory-paper, two cakes of 'Black Rose' soap (bright pink), a toothbrush and toothpaste, and a bottle of shampoo. A new phase was indeed beginning.

When he had gone my new head keeper (whom I called Spiderman, from the length and blackness of his limbs) asked me if there was anything I would like. So far I had made it a principle to ask for nothing, partly out of pride, to show them I was not to be got down by lack of luxuries, but mostly to avoid any need to feel beholden to them. But I decided that fresh air was not really a luxury, so I asked if I could have a window left open — even if it were only an inch — behind the bars. Spiderman said he would have to ask another man, the one who seemed to be in charge of the house and whom I called Charley-boy. But Charley-boy replied (in English, in front of me), 'I can't allow it.'

During the first two days of being locked up I came back again to thinking of Julius Caesar. Held for ransom, Caesar had laughed at the pirates when they named the sum they hoped to get for him, and said he was worth twice as much, sent off two servants to raise the money in nearby Rhodes, and settled down to make the best of life with the pirates while they and he waited. He made them play games and do athletics, and beat them soundly; read his own poetry aloud to them in the evenings and lectured or cuffed them if they failed to appreciate it, and told them that as soon as he was free he would raise a fleet, capture them in their turn, and have them all crucified. When the ransom was paid he did exactly as he had said he would.

I have never been entirely easy in my mind about this; not from fundamental objections to crucifixion but from a feeling that it was not altogether fair. He had told them the unvarnished truth; but still some sort of confidence must have grown up, and therefore a sense of betrayal been generated when the reckoning came.

Today hostages and kidnap victims are often urged to establish a personal relationship with their captors, in order to make it more difficult for these to kill them. Sympathies must be found and bonds created. But as I have already tried to explain, I had learned before the lagoon-crossing that that does not do. To set up any kind of friendly relations would have been a

98

form of begging for my life. Further, if I made them trust me I could not give information against them if I got out — which I had every intention of doing. I wondered once or twice whether I ought not to ignore such personal scruples (or pride), lead them to think I sympathized with their apish aims, learn all I could about them, and then persuade them to let me go by promising to give a good report of them to the outside world. Once free I could then shop them and justify it on the grounds that I had been under duress.

But it would not do. Caesar had been in quite a different position, I now saw.

Now that I had a table I asked Spiderman for an exercise-book to write in. He brought me one that night, and asked if I would also like books to read? He said he would try to bring me some, and I held down my hopes as best I could.

It was about this time that Kenyatta, asking me whether I knew that it was EROS whose hands I was in, added that its name had originally been EOS, from an ancient Greek word which, he said, I should no doubt know meant 'union' or 'unity'. (I had already owned to having lived in Greece and to knowing some Greek, for they had had to know why I was writing about it.) He said that the group's name had been changed from EOS — Eelam Organization of Students — to EROS — Eelam *Revolutionary* Organization of Students, as without the key word 'Revolutionary' people might fail to realize its true characteristic. I did not volunteer that the word *Eos* means 'dawn', or that the inclusion of 'dawn' in the titles of groups or publications generally shows their revolutionary politics. The less these people thought I knew about such things the longer my future was likely to be. But it interested me that this man, with his glorifying of Marxist theory and his belief that he was in the mainstream of world revolution, should know so little about it.

*

Being a prisoner teaches you that the smallest, most futile object has uses; and that your essential ally is discipline. You must make your own routine and stick to it.

I needed to keep my wits about me because interrogations happened at any time and always without warning. Therefore a reasonable amount of sleep was necessary. I had heard that long-term prisoners can train themselves to sleep for much of their time. I have always had insomniac tendencies so I could not do that, but I learned to impose on myself a regular four hours each night. How to fill the remaining twenty?

The two things that helped me most were poetry and a Persian vocabulary. I was lucky in having had an education which, although it had left me short on games and sciences, had given me a grounding in English literature and the habit of learning by heart. I was upset to find that I had forgotten a great deal that I had once known, but day by day more odd lines and verses kept coming back. If I had been locked in for long enough I might have finished up nearly as well furnished as when I set out.

My days began about 4 a.m., before first light showed fuzzily against the frosted glass, when what I supposed was the day-shift of terrorists took off on their motor-bicycles with a revving of engines echoing like chaos between the concrete walls. Once they were away I lay still and recited poetry to myself until six. Some poems can stand repetition again and again; others lose their meaning, or cloy. Some speak to you in the terms you most crave, exactly filling a hollow that has opened in your heart. Of all the authors I could call up, none did this for me so unfailingly or so well as Sir Walter Ralegh — I think because he looked so straight at fate. 'Blood shall be my body's balmer / No other balm shall there be given.' And with it his unquenchable delight in life. That poem was balm to me, and I said it every day. I did not want a poet who would fudge the issues. 'Walsinghame' rang as true; and the sonnet beginning 'Three things there be that prosper all apace / and flourish while they grow asunder far'; and great chunks of Shakespeare, for the same directness, though I cursed myself for the other great chunks that I had forgotten — perhaps because I had learned them too young to know what they meant.

And there was another category almost as potent: incantational poetry, that can lift you clean out of the real world into an ideal one. Shakespeare again; snatches of Milton and of Shelley; Keats's 'Ode to a Nightingale' (rather to my surprise: most of it is more direct than I had thought); Chesterton's 'Lepanto'; these were my mainstays. I had counted on both 'Kubla Khan' and 'The Rime of the Ancient Mariner', but they had not quite the necessary power when it came to it. They are the stuff of dreams, all right, but partly of bad dreams, and that may have been why they could not lift a payload. I would have given very much to be able to recite Virgil, but have never had the necessary grip of Latin. Odd snatches in translation came through, though, and of the Greeks, Pindar and Sophocles particularly, from the translations edited by Bowra and Higham.

Few poems served me better in its own way than 'Horatius on the Bridge'. Stirring and sustaining stuff as it is, it had the huge extra merit that to say it through takes thirty-five minutes. So when I felt — as I mistakenly did, sometimes — that I was at the end of my tether I would start to recite Horatius; I would emerge more than half an hour later with the illusion demolished, and reminded into the bargain of the value of never giving up. ('Now yield thee', cried Lars Porsena. 'Now yield thee to our grace.' Not on your nelly.)

The first two hours of the day ended with the arrival of tea. I had often contended that when I reach purgatory one of its afflictions will be compulsory, stewed, sweetened early-morning tea at 5 a.m. Imprisonment being not quite purgatory, Sambo did not appear with this stuff until some time between six and 6.30, but irrespective of him I got up at six and dressed.

It was impossible to make this activity last more than two minutes, as I had only three garments, but I could easily take up five minutes combing my hair with the pocket comb that had mystified the girl guerrilla. Then I made my bed — that is, laid the cloth absolutely smooth over it, folded my towel, which I used as a pillow, hung it on the bed-rail, and put the little hard bolster back in its place. (No one could possibly have slept on this object, but it was valuable to me as a back-rest, for as captivity went on I suffered more and more from an acutely aching spine: no doubt just the effect of a generally unhealthy life. I made myself do a few physical exercises every day, but got steadily more and more tired, so that before the end I could hardly stay sitting up without pain.)

Nasty as it was, I always drank Sambo's tea; partly in the belief that I needed the sugar, for energy (energy for what?), and partly because if I had not drunk it he might have ceased bringing it. Prisoners need as many punctuation-marks in their day as they can get. Then I would bang on my door to be taken to the washroom. The chairs in the hall where the duty-terrorists spent their time were in sight of both the wash-room door and mine, and there was nowhere between the two where I might have bolted, so I was allowed to come back on my own, the armed man merely getting up to lock my door again behind me. I found this a luxury for it gave me the sense, even if not the reality, of doing something of my own free will.

Then I read through what I had written the day before, correcting where I had room for it and keeping up elaborate counts of words to the line, to the page, to the chapter, and so on. I made sure that Spiderman and the others saw me, and told them what I was counting. In fact the counts had no purpose of their own, but they gave me some arithmetic to do and they sprinkled the page margins with figures. Into these I coded the dates, exact times, and directions of aircraft or helicopters going over, details which memory might soon mix up. Somebody's log-book, somewhere, would record the same figures, and if I got out with the book it would be possible to identify where I had been.

I was fed three times a day. I cannot say the food was good, but it was probably the same as their own, and Fuzzy and Sambo, who seemed to be responsible for it, did their best to make it appetizing. The rice was particularly disgusting: it had an overpowering smell like very dirty laundry. But when they could they gave me noodles instead, which were not nearly so bad, and all meals included those little bananas about three inches long which are so much better than the great pale sausages we import to this country. I think they were what I mainly lived on. Now and then one of my guards seeing an unemptied dish, would stare at me with his weapon pointing towards my stomach and demand: 'Hy you not eat? You must eat.' They never seemed to think it was not the way to give anyone an appetite. But I always answered that the food was very good: it was only that I was not hungry. For I knew that they could do no better and I had no wish to get underlings into trouble.

I ought perhaps to explain that the nicknames Fuzzy and Sambo were not meant to be in any way derogatory. I called Fuzzy so because he wore an Afro hair-style and devoted unflagging attention to it. Sambo was thick-lipped and bullet-headed, with half-scared, invincibly stupid eyes. The name presented itself; unsatisfactorily, but I lacked the energy to find one that fitted better. I have mentioned the way in which imagination dries up when your mind is occupied with practical problems of survival. I never addressed any of my gaolers by any name, but it irked me to be privately using names that would have seemed to them insulting had they known of them. Spiderman once instructed me to speak to them all as 'Comrade'. There is nothing comradely about a turnkey and I never did so; nor did any of them ever apply it to me. Towards the end they now and then addressed me as 'Madame'.

Once Spiderman asked me if I would like ice-cream, and I said yes. I realized my error a moment later when he revealed that one of the team (Fuzzy, it turned out) made the stuff himself. That night, beaming and squirming with pleasure, Fuzzy brought me a revolting cupful of fermenting squashed-up fruit out of a tin, stirred into condensed milk and a locally made sweetened fizzy-water which they all seemed very fond of. I had to eat several doses of this stuff, so as not to hurt his feelings.

Fuzzy tried very hard to produce meals in a European way, bringing a spoon and always wiping the bowl of it well with his thumb before he handed it to me. By the end of my stay he had more or less understood what a plate is for, though I doubt if he ever thought it sensible.

At ten every morning I banged on the door and went for the serious washing session of the day. This easily took up half an hour, often three-quarters, though not longer because the venue was neither clean nor sweet-smelling. The shower-pipe here was secured to the ceiling but the nozzle was missing, so that the water fell rather gratifyingly in a solid column. After some days I acquired two things which added greatly to my comfort: a spare cotton bed-cover (which I asked for and was reluctantly given) and a spare dress, brought unexpectedly by Kenyatta. I had to keep something on all night, since there was no telling when the door would crash open to admit an armed man and an interrogator. I had with me an Arab *shemagh* — which is simply a piece of thin, very loosely woven cotton about four feet square. Besides its basic use as a head-scarf it can serve as towel, tablecloth, cleaning-rag, screen, umbrella, almost what you will; only it is just not enough for decency, by itself. Now that I had the bed-cover I could use the *shemagh* as a nightdress — since the bed-cover was too dirty for direct contact. And I could now wash one item of clothing each morning under the shower, hang it to dry from the shelf I mentioned earlier, and put it on the next day only slightly damp. Hitherto I had had to wash my clothes at night, one item at a time, and put them back on in the morning still almost dripping wet.

Clothes-washing is crucial for prisoners under threat. Under interrogation you cannot control your sweat-glands. Each time the questioning got close to the bone I could smell the sweat of fear on myself; and although I knew that I was giving away nothing by eyes or hands or feet I would think: if one of these men knows anything about his business he will know he is on the right track; his nose will tell him. Not that I had anything much to conceal from them. But kidnappers are not basically reasonable men, and I found that rational responses were better not looked for in them.

Once the day's washing was done I wrote until lunch, over which I took as much time as I could. Then I lay down on my bed, not because I wanted or needed a rest but because it provided a change of position. The metal chair grew more uncomfortable day by day. This was the time for Persian practice. Three years before, looking unsuccessfully for a Pashto teacher, I had found a Persian lady in the village of Stenalees in Cornwall, and started taking Farsi lessons from her. After a month or two I ran out of money and had to stop, but she had got me the first reading-book for Class II in the primary schools. I had been a very slack and dull learner, but still I had by now got a rudimentary vocabulary and some idea of how a simple sentence is made. So I set myself daily to work through a part of the alphabet, trying to remember twenty words beginning with each letter, and keeping count on my fingers. I imposed rigid rules for this. No word could be counted if I did not know how to spell it, or was not sure what it meant, and not more than two words from the same verb or with the same prefix. It would have been more useful if I could have written my efforts down and compared one day's with the next, but I did not dare to. My gaolers would have thought it a code; and if they had realized it was Persian it would have cooked my goose for me, since they were all passionately pro-Iraqi. In either case they would have taken it as proof-positive that I was a spy after all. And they would have confiscated my exercise-book, a disaster too great to risk.

When I got weary of Persian I went over to Greek — and, as with poetry, was distressed to find how much I had forgotten. But one language or the other kept me going until four every afternoon. Then I got up, wrote until the light faded; went on writing if there was electricity, sat and ruminated or recited if there was not, until supper came — in its own time, and with a candle when needed. The electricity supply was erratic, to the high annoyance of the terrorists, who blamed the government's inefficiency for it although it was their fellows and rivals who were blowing up the line. Spiderman had a supply of thin, wobbly candles. He must have had a very accurate internal plumb-line: he could stick one on the used cap of a fizzy-water bottle so that, however bent the cap, the candle would stand straight and burn without guttering.

I went through another washing routine at 9.30, and at ten I went to bed, recited poetry for a short time, and then rehearsed Persian or Greek until about midnight, when I ordered myself to sleep. This ritual turned out to be hard to lose. For months afterwards, as soon as the light went out, a ribbon of words would begin to roll behind my closed eyelids and my mind would begin to enumerate: *bijan, bachche, bahar* or whatever, ready to keep it up for the next two hours.

Do these days sound dull? They were, but they were fairly often broken by interrogations, always without warning and often fairly unpleasant, but valuable because they were an insurance against apathy.

Just as the interrogators never said when they were really coming, so they often said they would come at a specific time, but never once did. It may have been part of a technique that they thought good. As they began to tire of trying to make me say I was an agent of MOSSAD, they turned to trying to link me with the South African organization BOSS; or failing that, the CIA, or MI5 or MI6. None of my interrogators seemed to have any contact with reality about this. My passport revealed my housewifely status and thorough Englishness, and no one I think could take me for anything else anyway. Why should I work as the agent of a foreign power with which I had no connection? I think they had absorbed so much current spy-fiction that they supposed the way of life it purports to describe must be common.

I grew tired of answering their endless questions, and said one day that there was, after all, something I did know about MOSSAD. They were agog; if they had had a tape-recorder handy they would certainly have brought it out. Yes? What could I tell them? I said: 'What I know is only from the Press; but it is that MOSSAD are very efficient: perhaps the most competent people of their kind in the world.' They nodded, their faces expressing their disgust as well as agreement, and anticipation of some devilish plot that I was now going to give away to them. I said: 'I'm sixty-four years old, a bit deaf, can't read without specs, and don't speak a word of Tamil. Do you really think that an organization like MOSSAD wouldn't employ someone better than me?' But it was days before they could bring themselves to accept this example of the blindingly obvious.

The day came when Spiderman appeared wearing the air of a successful conjuror at a children's party. 'I have brought you a book,' he said; and his eyes looked for, demanded, the gratitude which this time I could not have kept out of mine if I had tried. He put a dog-eared paperback down in front of me. It was James Hadley Chase's *No Orchids for Miss Blandish*.

This revolting tale describes a long-drawn-out kidnapping, and rams home two points: that once kidnappers have begun they are themselves trapped, there is no atrocity they will stop at before the end; and that when the victim is a woman the best her family can hope for is that she will not survive. It has been put to me that it can have been no accident that that was the first book I was brought. Someone chose it deliberately, as an aid to demoralization: a way of saying, this is what may happen if you don't co-operate. It is not impossible. I can visualize Kenyatta thinking along those lines. All the same, my own belief is that it was pure chance: one of those side-swipes that luck takes at us when the tide is running the wrong way anyhow.

On the day after my release an unknown American sent me a very beautiful bunch of orchids. I tried hard but unsuccessfully to contact this chivalrous stranger and thank him, not only for the flowers but for the fine twist of humour they added to this tale. If by chance he should read this book, I hope he will understand how much pleasure he gave me, and also enjoy the joke as much as I did.

I had never read *No Orchids* when Spiderman brought it to me; that is, I had read half of it when I was very young, but had given up because much of it I did not understand and the rest I neither liked nor believed. This time I read nearly all of it, simply because it was there, and was print. I found it very, very unpalatable. But before I had finished it Spiderman brought me a second book: a huge work on 'Problems of World Poverty' by a Swedish professor of economics, a Marxist when he began it. He wrote in American — I mean, in the convoluted, polysyllabic jargon of some American academics. If I had been given a choice I should surely not have picked it, for I know about as much of economics as a platypus may, and I like good English. But it had a merit that outweighed all its drawbacks: it was a hundred thousand words long. It was going to fill acres of time for me; every sentence would have to be read carefully, and many of them twice over to get their meaning, supposing that they had one. I read them so, in the days that followed, and long before the end I had become genuinely interested. Probably I knew not much more about economics by the end of it than I had at the start. But the Professor had begun by laying down the indisputable rightness of socialist solutions to his problems; and then, as he detailed one disastrous Third World experiment after another, led his readers with academic honesty at last to the conclusion that those solutions do not work and never can.

To be given such a book by my devotedly Marxist captors was interesting. It was obvious that Spiderman and the others in the house would not have read it: they had not enough English to get through a page, and almost certainly had read neither Marx nor any other serious writer, in any language. But what did the book tell about the people who had lived here before, to whom the house (and the books) had probably belonged? Once or twice on my way back from the washroom last thing at night, I glimpsed a very old man squatting on the floor wearily grinding spices for next day's curry; and I once saw a youngish woman (who I think cooked for them all) with a child and a baby. These people were treated as servants, and I had the impression that I was not supposed to know of their existence.

As the weeks went on I saw half a dozen or more of the books that had been left behind here. Bernard Shaw's plays; Ignazio Silone's *Seed beneath the Snow* in an English translation; D. H. Lawrence's *The White Peacock*; Malcolm Muggeridge's *Tread Softly*; the others escape me now. But they, and the house, built up a picture of a wealthy English-educated family who had started on the far Left and moved steadily — like the Swedish professor — towards reality. Was that why they had lost their house to the *bandar-log*? And what had happened to them? Had they simply been turned out 'in the People's name'? Had they been stood against a wall? I often wondered, while the nights spun slowly away to the incessant click of the Kalashnikov rifles being proved and re-proved: almost the only pastime, it seemed, that these sad and vicious children knew.

All this time it was really Spiderman's exercise-book that was keeping me sane.

I suppose it is hard for newcomers now to imagine Olympia without many hundreds or even thousands of people in it. And it stands over enough ground to soak up a crowd; no doubt there were a few thousands there when the Games first began. But places cannot give you all that they hold, when they are being swarmed over like carcasses by ants. They have their ways of speaking, but it is done in a very low voice.

I had kept my hopes of Olympia in check after Delphi, because it is not healthy to expect too much when the standard has already been set very high. Besides, I knew that Olympia lay in a flat valley, and it is mountains that set my head on fire. (I had made a similar idiot's error when I supposed, because the Greek and Roman inheritances move me more than the Gothic, that I should not be carried clean away by Chartres Cathedral.) It remains impossible to compare Delphi and Olympia, any more than you can compare Chartres with St Mark's. They come from different endeavours of the human spirit, and work different purposes. I have never found any place that gives so strongly the sense of having been holy, for so long, as Delphi. Not that there are not older shrines, but God was not in them, or has departed; and it is occupation, not nominal possession, that leaves its trace. Delphi for me is possibly the most beautiful and evocative place on earth. Yet Olympia is scarcely less so. Perhaps they ought always to be seen one after the other in a short space of time, for between them they evoke the two great streams of Greek thinking, the spiritual and the political, on which all our lives are tossed backwards and forwards, down to this day.

Delphi saw the first desperate climb out of darkness into sunlight; the shaking-off of the terrible and disgusting earth-goddesses, of the snake and the pig, human sacrifice, menstrual blood and necromancy. Men were stumbling out into free air: mind instead of entrails, sunlight and medicine instead of witchcraft and the bowels of the earth. It was a very long haul; the Pythoness was still chewing her hallucinatory leaves after Aristotle had written his *Natural Philosophy* and Eratosthenes had measured the earth. Nor is it over yet. People with transistor radios can be found today killing cocks and conjuring with fetid

110

substances in churchyards, while others meekly kill themselves by the hundred on a maniac's order because he is black and wakes in them a primeval awe of darkness and earth. But in so far as we have free use of mind today, and can think and reason and reach outwards instead of inwards, we owe it to the Greeks: we are still running on the scent that they picked up. And Delphi is one of the places where that hunt started.

Olympia is quite different: it holds the chart of our political progress. It saw the rise of the notion that gods and men alike can come together in amity as well as in war; that differences can be sunk; above all that strength resides in law and order, that the wheatfield is worth more than the cave. Olympia talks about greatness and prosperity and quiet, though its voice is not easy to hear amongst the motor-horns and clamour, the touts and guides and cigarette packets and physical congestion of today. Delphi speaks in a rougher voice, not to the intellect searching for political order but to the spirit battling against the gut.

When I first came to Olympia there were a few sightseers there but not enough to silence it. Since the end of the war little tidying-up had been done on any of the archaeological sites, and most of them, including Olympia, were still unfenced. There was no difficulty in keeping out of the way of the few little groups being escorted round by ciceroni, or of the occasional youth with a rucksack and a *Guide Bleu*. But during the years under occupation there had been a steady flow of Italian and Germanic *Kultur*-seekers, and this had left its mark on the manners of the place. The morning was all right, but in the afternoon, when work and school were over and elders were safely sleeping, a handful of boys and young men began to roam the site seeking whom they might annoy. So I was glad when, climbing through a gap in a wall, I came on a party of five or six obviously English people including an elderly woman in a floppy hat and flowing silks (apricot-coloured, as I can still see, against the dazzling stones and cool darkness of the pines).

I asked if I might join them for a few minutes, until the boys had found something else to distract them. They were most kind, and urged me to come round the rest of the site, for they had a very distinguished archaeologist with them, and rightly said that it would be a shame for me to miss the chance of listening to him. Presently one of them nodded towards the woman and said: 'You know who this is, don't you?' And then, surprised that I had not guessed: 'It's Freya Stark.'

I was not impressed, for a very stupid reason which I ought to have been ashamed of then, and am now. My father knew her slightly and I had heard him speak of her, but only with impatience and scorn. He thought that, unable to get herself noticed in other ways, she was driven by vanity to do things she should have had more sense than to try, and he then had to send aeroplanes to get her out of trouble. (I do not believe that this had happened often; but I suppose it must have happened at least once, and then multiplied in his mind.) My father supposed that no woman ever had any motive for her actions but desire to attract the attention of men. He thought this natural and laudable. But for a woman voluntarily to undergo hardship in dirty conditions seemed to him thoroughly unattractive, therefore whoever did it must be stupid. As for any value that Freya Stark's expeditions might have had in themselves, that was a stupid idea too. If facts were needed about desert places, any man could collect them a great deal better and without wasting other people's time.

Having heard these things about her, I simply assumed that I should find them myself.

Only one hotel was open in Olympia and Freya was staying there. She assumed that I was, too, but it was too expensive for me; I had found a room in a house at the other end of the village. She invited me to dinner, and I accepted gladly, but for some perverse reason I decided not to give away that I knew who she was. I washed the dust out of my hair and put on my still clean spare shirt and walked up to the hotel, wondering what sort of evening to expect.

I had thought that the rest of the party would be there, but she had arranged for us to dine alone except for one: I believe he was the British Consul from Patras. She was a delightful hostess, managing to give the impression that she was genuinely interested in her chance guest, and taking the trouble to interest me in endless ways. Presently she began asking in detail where I had been and what I had done or thought. Then she wanted to know where next? Bassae, for which the starting-point was and is Andritsaina. How far away was that? Some thirty-five miles as the crow flies. She supposed there would be a bus I could take. I explained that the distance by road was sixty miles, and I would much rather walk thirty-five miles, enjoying every step, than spend four hours in a bus. She agreed; but could I walk thirty-five miles in a day? I thought probably not; but I could lie down and sleep wherever I came to. Yes; and I was bound to get off track, so the distance might be more like fifty miles in the end. Could I carry enough water, as well as food, for two days? This has always been one of my weak points. I can walk for a very long time, but not carrying a load. I said doubtfully that I did not know, but that the only way to find out was by trying.

And so on. Presently Freya suggested diffidently that it might be best and most enjoyable to hire a horse. Probably it would not cost very much. The Consul was asked, and turned out to be of the right kind, for he knew. It would be the equivalent of £2 and that would include the man who would have to go too, to bring the horse back. He advised me to go out early in the morning to a village beyond Olympia, ask there for the schoolmaster (because he would be a village dignitary who could arrange such things, and also he would have some English or French), offer Dr. 100,000, and let the schoolmaster find the horse and the man and endorse the bargain.

There was much other talk, all of it fascinating for me. As I walked back to my room at last my mind was in a great muddle of delight and remorse. For not once in the whole

113

evening had Freya spoken a syllable to suggest that she was anything of a traveller, or experienced in overcoming difficulties in rough places. I had supposed her to be silly and vain because I had heard her called so, and she had shown me that she was exactly the opposite, and kind and charming into the bargain. That was what I felt the remorse for, and I made a resolve never again to prejudge anyone on hearsay, no matter how good the source. Of course I have done so endless times since; but I still try not to.

A dozen years later, when I was in Cyprus, Freya wrote and asked me to go round Crete with her, as she did not know it and I did. I have rarely felt so honoured. But I was under contract to the Red Cross and with no leave owing to me, so I had to refuse, and have always regretted it. We miss so many things for no reason except that they come at the wrong times. But no doubt the brickbats miss us too for the same reason, so it would be wrong to complain.


You can see more of the country from a horse's back than on Shanks's pony; and apart from the extra views, you do not have to watch where your feet are going. The horse does that for itself, and you can watch the birds, the rise and fall of the mountains like clouds, and the clouds like mountains, and not finish up on your face in the myrtle.

Between Olympia and Andritsaina the sacred river Alph has to be forded several times. It runs in many channels, some of them thigh-to-waist deep in summer and probably uncrossable in winter or early spring, when the snow-water is coming down off Mount Vermioni. This too makes it all the more desirable to be on a horse.

Andritsaina turned out to be a large, prosperous village, almost a town: very attractive to look at, and with a fountainhead in the square completely enclosed by the trunk of a plane tree, gigantic and immensely old, so that the tree itself seemed to be pouring out living water to whoso might be in need. Yet something rang wrong in the place. There was a faint but discernible taint on the air of greed and hostility and desire to be modern, that I had met nowhere else. Perhaps the inhabitants had been on the wrong side in the Civil War, and were still smarting. Perhaps the buses bearing sightseers to Bassae had already proved malignant. There was one bus there when I arrived, but it was not the most virulent kind: twenty-nine Belgian students had hired it between them and, in the charge of a finals-year man, were taking it as far as they could.

There was a café in the square, with rooms for tourists above; where there were facilities of that kind it seemed a duty to use them, for the sake of others coming after. For if not, those who had had the enterprise to open such places would think it not worth while after all, and give up. That by staying open they might be contributing to the destruction of their country's true quality and therefore long-term good, was too complicated an equation for an ignoramus from abroad such as myself to work out.

I took a room and went to lie down in it; in ten minutes I found that there was an eye on the other side of an inch-wide gap in the plank door. I went out on to the landing and scowled at the two figures sauntering away. Five minutes later the eye was back. I went downstairs and asked the proprietor to have the peeping Toms removed. He looked very angry; I guessed that one peeping Tom was probably his son. I went and sat outside with a cup of coffee. The horse's owner was loading up a huge sack of some substance which he had come here to fetch. Inspired no doubt by the atmosphere of the place he said that he wanted another Dr.20,000. I reminded him that he had agreed the price with the schoolmaster. Yes, he said; but it had turned out to be further than he had thought. But he had been here before? And was coming here anyway, to fetch his sack? He fell back on simply repeating what he wanted, though with not much conviction. The café proprietor and customers looked on. I could not afford any more, being not less hard-up than he was. I did a lot of dictionary-work while they waited, and then said: 'I am ashamed that you, the Hellenes, try to cheat foreigners.' So was he; he got up and walked away. Someone sent a glass of wine to my table, but I was tired of Andritsaina.

This was the only place in which I ever found either scrupulous honesty or courtesy lacking. I remember it only as the one plantain that emphasizes the lovely texture of the grass.

Just before dark, when the Belgians reappeared, they asked me to join them on their bus. They were going to Mycenae, then back to the Piraeus to ship the bus to Crete. I went with them.

They were a charming lot, high-spirited and full of enthusiasm, doing their best to see the life of the country, and to like the food, and not to mind the dust and heat; and they were making a good job of it. They were all interested in ancient Greek history and some of them in modern history too. They were generous: when they asked me to come with them it was on the understanding that as I had no sleeping-bag three girls with blankets would put them down side by side and the result would be plenty of cover for four. I have thought the better of Belgium ever since. In return, I could be of some slight use to them, for the Greeks often could not understand their English; and though none of us had enough Greek to spit on, I had marginally more than they, and a freer notion of how to use it. I could also brief them slightly about local customs, which they were anxious to treat with respect.

But after two days I knew I should not be going to Crete with them. Pleasant as their company was, I saw that in it I should not learn the sort of things that I longed to know. They were cut off, by the bus and by each other, from half of what they had come to see: from everything, in fact, except the classical sites. You do not see out of a dust-filled window at 30 m.p.h. the same things as you do on foot. When thirty people are talking round you, you do not hear many other voices. And you cannot learn much about how other people's lives are led unless — at least a few times — you sit at their hearths. So with regret I left them at Karytaina and set off by myself again.

Sadly there is no escaping the rule that, though travelling in rough or lonely places is very much pleasanter with friends than alone, very much less comes of it. So it is a matter of choice — as with all things worth doing.

Against buses themselves I have nothing to say. It is only when they produce isolation that they do not serve. Local buses do not cut you off from local life, they carry it along with them; and there is no better place for working at a language, since everyone within range will want to have a go at the foreigner, and you can open up the dictionary on your knee and work from it without having to stop — as you must if you are walking. Still, foot-travel is the most enjoyable of all, until you are too tired to be more than half-conscious. Then you can slump on to a bus seat and appreciate it as a luxury.

I have done no long-distance walking in England: rarely as much as a day. One reason is that in one's own country, and one's own clumsily congested life, enough time is not often to spare. It all gets frittered in odd ten minuteses. But a much more compelling reason is that, except in a very few places, England is too crowded. Even out of season it is difficult to go a mile without passing people or houses and attracting curious looks. And I have never been able to outgrow a childish shyness about that, which makes me uncomfortable. I know that no one is interested, and that strangers' minds are on their own and each other's business, not on me, but still I feel as if censorious eyes were boring into my back as I pass.

In Greece in the 1950s there was no way of moving about the countryside except by walking, so no one could possibly have thought it odd. But also you could walk for half a day and see no one; and when you did see someone he would come up and speak his curiosity frankly, and you could explain.

I am not generally afraid of my fellow men once face to face with them, and have found no reason for being so at a slight remove. No doubt it is all due to some form of guilt, and any psychologist could identify it.

Why does memory yield me so little now of the rest of that journey? In Mystras I stayed in a village house beside a convent of great charm whose Mother Superior, equally charming in a different way, spoke good French and told me much about the ruins. I know of few places where there is so strong a sense of arrested time. Here was a great and pious glory, and the Frankish mailed fist came down upon it and did not destroy it, neither did the despots of the Morea, but the Turks blotted it out. I remember one of those moments when for an instant your blood seems to run backwards, as I came up the steep track, once a paved road, into a square. Before me was a roofless church. The inside walls in the falling sunlight dripped with red and blue and gold, all the glory of Byzantium glowing there; and through the round, exquisite arch of a window a donkey looked out at me. 'This place,' said its rough limbs and tattered ears and dark, wary eyes, 'is better suited to me, now, than to any of you.'

I remember the great beauty of the plain of Sparta, and the charmlessness of the town itself, carrying not a trace of past glory. But perhaps that is right, for it was the wrong kind of glory anyway and did not deserve to last. And the dark, brooding silence of Mycenae: as desolate as Mystras, but with its secrets still locked up inside it, not picked white by the crows as Mystras is. Of how I got back to Athens I have no recollection at all.

Rereading these notes I find that I can remember much that eluded me when I was writing the last paragraph. So why was memory not serving me efficiently at the time?

I had finished the day's work and turned in for the night, and had been lying composed on my planks for about an hour when I heard my door being unlocked; one of my interrogators was let in: the one I called Lobster-Eyes. He questioned me for two hours or more, going again and again over ground covered in other sessions. But at the end he made a change. He asked me: 'What do you think we are going to do with you?' I had grasped at least one rule about interrogations: always say the truth unless a lie is necessary; it saves a lot of confusion. So I said, 'I suppose you'll kill me.' He answered, 'We may not kill you; but we want a lot more information out of you.'

I had been ready to be shot since all this began; but stupid as it may sound I had not, until he said that, thought seriously about being tortured. Now that it did occur to me the prospect worried me very much. I did not – still do not – know whether under such conditions I could go on behaving as I ought; and I was even more afraid of a failure of that kind than I was of pain or disfigurement. It was a bridge I could not cross before I came to it, but for a time the thought of it interfered with the pleasures of recollection.


Kenyatta told me to write a letter to Tony, which he said he would post. Hope generates belief; I did so, and the letter was read carefully by Spiderman and then by Kenyatta; but since it told them nothing they wanted to know they did not trouble even to carry it away. It did, however, give me a brief glimpse into Spiderman's view of life.

My son had got engaged just before I had gone to Sri Lanka and the wedding had been fixed for March 31st. I was afraid the bride's family, and the young couple, would feel that they must postpone it if they had heard nothing of me, or heard that I was dead; it is very easy to feel guilty about

119

being happy when one's near and dear are in a hole. I felt guilty from the opposite angle: for spoiling, through my predicament, what should be a time of perfect happiness for them. I knew Tony would understand this, and in my letter I urged him not to allow any change of plans.

When Spiderman had read it he looked puzzled and slightly upset.

'You don't want to be at the wedding?'

'Yes, of course I do.'

'Then hy you tell them not to wait?'

'I want them to be happy. They're young; it's hard to wait when you're young.'

Spiderman looked thoroughly disapproving. 'Not good. They should wait. For the mother.'

'But they might have to wait a long time.'

'Yes. But they should.'

I wondered what marriage actually meant to this doctrine-crazed young man. I think he was reacting purely in terms of bourgeois social niceties. Later he asked me abruptly whether I believed in God. I said yes; then added: 'You are an atheist?'

'Yes,' he said, sounding uncomfortable, as if the question had been tactless or the subject were improper. Yet it was he who had raised it.


Books transformed my day's routine, though I had to ration myself so as not to run the well dry. I read between breakfast and ablutions, and for a good part of the afternoon. In the evening if there was electric light I read between supper and bedtime; if not, I recited or wrote, since writing is easier by candlelight than reading.

I read as slowly as I could, and with meticulous attention. I had not tried Shaw since adolescence (when I had admired him vastly), but the plays turned out to be shallow and class-ridden, recalling his own definition (in *The Intelligent Woman's Guide*, I think) that 'socialism is about class'. What a trivial preoccupation for a live mind. Lawrence was equally obsessed by it, in an even more stultifying way, seeing it, through clouds of envy, almost as a suit of clothes; though he was a fine descriptive writer. I suppose the subject seemed important in the changing social climate of the turn of the century, but in the long run it has turned out to be very small beer.

Silone's outrage at the Italian peasant's lot still rang true and tragic, throwing into chilling light the cruelty of the Communist betrayal. If only these self-styled freedom-fighters could have read him, I sometimes thought, their compatriots might be spared a lot of suffering. But that was unrealistic of me. The murder and mayhem of the Tamil 'liberation struggle' were ordered not for the love of men (it is hard to kill where you love) but for personal power; the corruption at the heart of the theories of revolution is nothing to such people. This was true right down to the level of those who interrogated me and claimed the power of life and death over me: Kenyatta, Lobster-Eyes and the others. It was not the fires of compassion that burned in their bellies, but the fires of ambition and self-importance. As for the small fry, they had fetched up swimming in this muddy pool because they could not keep afloat in a better one. Some were subnormal, one or two unbalanced, the others no more than mindlessly besotted with self-admiration. Vanity was the outstanding characteristic of them all. Charley-boy was a degenerate, Fuzzy on the edge of being what the Cornish call 'not 'xactly'.

As well as searching my handbag they kept asking me again and again whether I had got jewels or money. I had been careful to set out only with enough cash for the petrol I should need, and a meal, and a hundred rupees (about three pounds) for contingencies. What was left of this small sum was counted and put back endless times, and always whoever put it back pointed out to me that he had done so. Mao, I remembered, was adamant that the People's Army must not steal from their victims. I had little doubt that if I had had a large sum on me, or valuable jewellery, they would have 'confiscated' it, telling me that it was not for themselves, it was for 'the Cause'. But I think they were afraid of being accused of petty stealing, and kept a close watch on each other against it.

One of them (it was Lobster-Eyes, I think) one day fixed his attention on my wedding-ring.

'That is gold?'

'Yes.'

'You have gold jewellery, yes?'

'Every Christian woman has such a ring from her husband. It's the sign of marriage.' I was sure that he knew this.

'Show me.' He reached out for it.

I said: 'No Christian woman ever takes it off. Her husband or her son takes it, only when she's dead.' We stared at each other across the corner of the table. I would have fought for it, and he must have seen in my eyes that I would. He would have got it, of course; but it is not entirely easy to pull a ring off by force, and I suppose he had no authority from Madras to start a rough-house. After a few moments' silence he went on to something else.

I learned more about Spiderman than about the others, because of his English. He said that his father had been a government servant under the British, and that he went to see the old man once a month. I got the impression that Marxism and Eelam were not enthusiasms they could share. Spiderman made repeated attempts to set up friendly relations with me. (It may be that he was under orders to do so and had been picked as likely to succeed. He was tall and handsome as Tamils go.) I think he never understood why I did not respond.

He seemed as disconnected from reality as the interrogators. One evening (it was diversions such as this that kept me going from week to week) I was just finishing my writing stint when he burst in. There had been a long interrogation that day, all aimed at getting information out of me about the security forces: what weapons I had seen them with, where I had seen army posts, whether bridges or culverts were guarded, and the like. I had been the quintessential fool throughout, not knowing an armoured personnel carrier from a bullock-cart and never having lifted my eyes from the pot-holes in the road-surface as I drove along. I had got used to this role, and thought it a bit much that Spiderman should now be set to go on with the interrogation.

'Bridge,' he shot at me. 'You know bridge?'

'What bridge?'

'You know.'

This is of course one of the most often-repeated phrases of interrogators (anyway of bad ones). I began a rambling, damn-fool statement to show that I was hardly up to knowing what a bridge is for. But Spiderman cut me short, flinging down in front of me a grubby booklet:

TEN EASY LESSONS IN CONTRACT BRIDGE

'You show me.' And he slammed down a pack of cards beside it.

From PK I had learned my lesson: never to laugh when it is not expected. I solemnly dealt out four hands, faced them, sorted them; bid on them, played them through.

'Do again.'

I did. The third time round he began to reach out and play cards himself, from any of the hands. Then he swept them all together, with the booklet. 'Now, I know,' he said gruffly, and clanked out.

'A year before I ever came to Greece I wrote a story about a British officer fighting with Zervas' guerrillas against the Germans in the last war, badly wounded and brought in to a monastery to live or die. Convalescing, he learned that the monks ran a dressing station for the Resistance; he added a messenger service, taught them how to use a radio, maintain

123

weapons, make up plastic explosive charges, and so on. But in the meantime the monks were at work on him and he began to feel the pull of the life of holiness and quiet. With the end of the war he found nothing but disillusionment at home: the girl he loved had married someone else, everything had become tawdry and trivial. He decided to take the Orthodox faith, go back to the monastery, and live there. But he found that he had himself destroyed what he was looking for. The community had broken up, the abbot now held a commission in the Greek Army, the one truly saintly monk was dead, and the building had been taken over by the military.

I did not know enough about Greece, or Orthodoxy, or irregular warfare, to make a success of this. But I tried hard, for I have always hoped and sometimes believed that thorough homework can make up for all deficiencies. And to help keep my topographical details consistent I picked a spot on the map for my imaginary monastery.

The day came when I found myself on the way to Konitsa near the Albanian frontier. The site for my fictional monastery was not much off my route, and to my delight I heard that there actually was a monastery there. I was set down from a country bus at a spot where a very small footpath crossed the road, and was told to follow it for a few miles until the belfry came in sight. Only, why did I want to go there? I had no hope of explaining that; and as I set off I was conscious of leaving doubt and perplexity behind me.

The path wound in and out of hills slippery with rain. There were sharp scents in the air. Spring comes late in the northern Pindus, with small starry flowers that have sheltered through the winter under snow. I caught a glimpse of a bell-tower but it vanished again behind a hill. Then I came round a shoulder, and there high above me stood a great building part destroyed and part repaired. Below it, in huge letters of white stones across the hillside, ran the words: CHRIST IS RISEN; WE WANT THE ARMY — as if the one thing followed from the other.

Out of the valley floor a greasy clay path climbed past a

124

sentry-box. The man inside said yes, this was the right path to the monastery. I had already from far off seen a large flat space of bare soil gouged out of the hillside. Now as I came over a scarp I saw fifty men drilling on it; behind them a line of vehicles parked, and beyond these, unmistakable mule-lines. At the gate a child ran out and urged me to go on up to the door itself. It was opened by a youngish woman with a toddler peeping from behind her. Yes, she said, it was the monastery door; the abbot was out at present, but I must come in. The abbot would be delighted to welcome a guest and a stranger, and would certainly insist that I stay overnight.

She put me first in the guest-parlour, then came back and led me into a long, high room completely filled with books — on shelves all round the walls, on tall, free-standing bookcases down the room, as in college libraries, in piles on the floor, Amongst them was a bed, and she gently but firmly put me down on it as if I had been a child. I gave in to this because it was now siesta time, and to break customs is only to make a nuisance of oneself to other people. But I blamed myself that I had not yet got enough Greek to read what lay all round me. What may not have been there?

About half-past four the young woman took me to wash, gave me delicious fresh milk, quite unlike the thin fluid usually produced by Greek cows, then led me outside to drink tea (a most un-Greek procedure) with the abbot. He was a fine-looking man in his late thirties or early forties, and he had good English. The monastery had changed radically in the last seven years, he said. Zervas' guerrillas had used it during the war, and he had fought along with them. The Germans had partly destroyed the place during their retreat, hence the rebuilding; and then during the civil war the army had taken it over. It was they who had taught him to drink tea like the English. Now the monks were allowed to carry on in this small part of it, but there were only four of them left. He himself, with one of them who had studied agriculture, was trying to set up a modern farm on the monastery land. Would I not like to see over it?

It was a brave effort, and looked successful. He had imported immense, mouse-coloured Swiss cows. Would they thrive here? Well, he said, he had thought these mountains were not too unlike the Swiss Alps. And he showed an excellent lucerne crop coming up for them. There was a modern-looking piggery, a milking-parlour, corn and barley, alfalfa, and four acres of young fruit trees. At the end of the tour he returned me to the young woman, with instructions to deliver me to the refectory for dinner at 8 o'clock.

In due time she led me to a big square room with a stone-flagged floor and fine vaulting carried on two lines of squat columns down the room. A great many candles were burning. (The military side of the establishment ran a generator but the abbot rightly preferred candle-light.) Between the columns stood a long, dark wood refectory table, laid with silver and glass for nine. And at the further end of the room were Turkish-style low stone divans piled with red and purple cushions much trimmed with gold. A roaring log fire burned on a wide stone hearth.

The diners assembled slowly: the commander of the unit stationed here; the district commander, making an inspection tour; an agriculturist and a water surveyor up from Athens; a senior doctor preparing a report on health in the area; the abbot, and two other monks. We reclined among the braided cushions while ouzo and *mezedakia* were served to us by a deacon. The atmosphere was that of, say, dinner with the Wali of Swat in 1906: the fighting has ceased but everyone is conscious of being in a frontier-zone; the men of war are the allies and protectors of the men of peace, and the West is looked to not for modernity but for order and civilized ease.

At table I was put between the district commander and the doctor, and the commander reminisced about the war. No, he had not been here then, but he had heard that an English parachutist had persuaded the monks to play an active part. The junior officer listened, and now and then chipped in. He was twenty-two, he had missed all of the war itself, but seen a bit of the civil war. That was something that must never be allowed to happen to these wretched people again, but the danger was still there. He looked significantly northwards. God be thanked that there was a military presence up here.

The doctor spoke excellent French. He thought the story about the English parachutist was probably true; nowadays people were apt to put an Englishman into any exploit being talked of, but very often they were right about it.

He said there was a lot of tuberculosis in the area, and still a distressing rate of malnutrition, but the mountain air was very healthy and diseases were few. The real scourge was Malta fever. There was not a cow from here to the sea that was not infected, including the abbot's prized Swiss imports. 'It's magnificent milk,' he said, 'and they'll try to make you drink it for breakfast. Don't touch it: it's absolutely deadly.'

Meantime course was succeeding course, piled on great Victorian china dishes and served by two deacons and the young woman, while an old crone supervised a charcoal fire in a doorway in the background. I said to the doctor: 'I find it harder every minute to be sure whether all this is real, and really happening, or whether I'm dreaming it.' His face lit with pleasure. 'That's what I've been asking myself all evening,' he said. 'But since we're both dreaming it, perhaps it's real.'


I had been to Iannina before, going by village buses up through Thessaly to the monasteries of the Meteora — that mighty cluster of limestone rocks rising sheer for hundreds of feet into the air, like chimney-pots, at the head of the plain. The monastic orders made hermitries there, living on ledges and in caves (some of them little bigger than dog-kennels) in the face of the rock, like seagulls nesting. Then, towards the close of the fourteenth century, fearing destruction by the Turks, they piled up like ravens' nests five great monasteries on the flat tops, and provisioned and armed them like the fortresses they were. Until the 1930s the Great Meteora could only be reached in a net pulled up by rope from the top, a final haul of 120 feet.

I was sad to have missed this way of ascent myself: a Jacob's ladder of steps has been cut (some sections tunnelled right into the rock), and visitors are now compelled to use it. But the net was still in use for fetching up supplies.

From the Meteora the old road to Iannina climbs into the hills and over the Metsovo pass. It was only thanks to the Germans having metalled it for their military traffic that we could get along here at all. There were prepared places for passing; and other places where the conductor would get down and measure up, and signal the driver on inch by inch; and others again where the driver would put his foot flat down on the accelerator and all the passengers would clutch the rail of the seat in front with one hand, and cross themselves right-to-left with the other.

I had heard a lot about Thessaly as a great and fertile plain, wheat-growing, lush from the edge of the broad river-lawns to the brink of the dewy caves, and so on. When I saw it, it seemed small in size and it did not look to my western wet-land eyes as if there were enough grass on it to keep a flock of geese for a week. (Probably there was not, for it was early September and no rain had fallen for months.) I could nowhere see a patch of ground that in England anyone would have imagined was cultivable. And yet I could see cultivation everywhere; sometimes a few vegetables, sometimes a little strip of wheat stubble no more than a few hands wide among the stones, that would have been reaped with one of the little sickles, six or seven inches across, that hung in the village shops. And there were fruit trees, which suggested that the place would look better in the spring. Most of Greece, I thought, is one great stone-heap; and I was lost in admiration for the race that has wrung a living out of it for the last 3,000 years.

It says in the *Golden Ass* that all the women of Thessaly are witches. I had read this as a child, and forgotten all about it, and it came back to me now with great force because I saw that nearly all the women there did indeed look like witches;

handsome ones, many of them, and a few very beautiful, but with flashing black eyes and hook noses, and looking more than capable of tearing a man's throat out and putting an enchanted sponge in its place, so that he does not know what she has done to him until he is far away and tries to drink at a stream.

At the Meteora there were no witches and not many monks either, but there was a test of morale. At the top of the steps leading to the Great Meteora, there is a wide and pleasing terrace laid out on the flat top of the rock; and there I was greeted with great courtesy by a grey-bearded and venerable abbot. It is the baseline of hospitality in Greece to offer the arriving stranger a drink of water before anything else. This charming old man called for, and carried to me, a glass brimming with liquid of a slightly pinkish or sandy-grey colour, very pale. Midway in it was suspended a kind of thickening: not a lump, not sediment, for that would have gone to the bottom, but more what one might suppose ectoplasm to be like, or the frog that forms in a cider barrel, only not so solid. I opened my mouth to say I was not thirsty (a lie that no one could possibly have believed) but lost my nerve, took the glass, and, playing for time, asked whether there was a rock-spring somewhere up here. No, the abbot said. The monastery had been built in 1367, in faith that God would always preserve the community from all ills including death by thirst. They had cut cisterns in the rock, which filled every winter, and every winter since then God had sent enough rain to last the monks until He pleased to send them more. This year there had been a dry spring and the summer had been hot. The cisterns were low. But if necessary God would send a freak shower to carry them on till the autumn storms. It had often been so in the past.

If holy water is water blessed by the faith of men, I thought, there is only one thing I can do. I shut my eyes, drank off the glassful, and said it was delicious. And God rewarded me with no ill effects at all.

*

The next bus was full of soldiers. At the top of the Metsovo Pass everyone was turned out while the driver took the bus backwards down to a hut where petrol was sold out of drums (there was no filling-station on the road, as now). The soldiers put up a cigarette packet on a pine trunk and began target practice; one of them asked if I could hit it, and handed me his rifle. I did hit it, and for the rest of the trip they sang celebratory songs such as foreigners might like. These were plaintive and merry and violent, and some of them very oriental. But the only one I have ever been able to remember is 'Yerakina' — the girl whose bracelets clashed like thunder, and who fell into the well.

There were no new buildings in Iannina then, or none to notice. The narrow little streets of overhanging houses still had a Turkish twist; where they opened up they gave glimpses of one of the town's two little mosques, and the effect was like an Edward Lear painting, only that the figures were more shabbily dressed. One of these mosques is built on the very end of a low cliff jutting out into the lake, its minaret against the skyline and a fringe of untended bushes fluffing up round it like a nest around a moorhen.

A very ancient boatman rowed me across to the island in the middle of the lake where Ali Pasha's palace still stands. It is not very palatial, but in a melancholy way immensely attractive, and still reveals the inexplicable would-be scholar and patron of the arts in the otherwise wholly Albanian tyrant and murderer. He served the Turks with flagitious cunning and ferocity till he had almost become an emperor on his own, made an alliance with Napoleon, then with the British, and was murdered on the lake island, at Sultan Mahmud II's orders, in 1822.

As we rowed back the frogs in the lake began to chorus: 'Brek-ek-ek-ek, ko-ax, ko-ax', and the aged boatman did indeed seem to be keeping time with them, as in Aristophanes. He began to talk: such was his consciousness of his own age that he half-believed he could actually remember Ali Pasha. He told the tale of Kyra Phrosini, the beautiful young Greek girl

whom Ali Pasha took (among others) for his harem. At first
the Greeks despised her for not having killed herself: but gradually they saw that she had gone in order to try to save her
fellow citizens and tame the tyrant's taste for murder. She
saved many lives and eased the weight on many others. In the
end Ali Pasha understood what she had been doing, and had
her strangled and her body thrown into the lake. But she had
become a heroine to her own people. The boatman said re-
verently: 'All the women of the town came to the shore and
poured their sugar into the lake. Why did they do that, do
you think? I'll tell you. So that Kyra Phrosini should drink
sweet water even in her grave.' I hope that the old man himself
is drinking it now.

One day Spiderman came in, a good deal agitated, to tell me
it was being said on the radio that the government was about
to bomb Jaffna. I said: 'They haven't got any bomber aircraft,
have they?' I knew they had not, and thought he probably
knew it too; but by now I was used to Tamils' capacity to
believe absolutely anything, even against the evidence of their
own eyes. Charley-boy and Spiderman had portable radios,
fixed so that they received only Madras and a Soviet service
in English. I knew this because Spiderman had twice left his
briefly with me so that I might hear Moscow being scornful
about the British government. So now I knew too that he had
heard this false rumour from either Madras or Moscow. This
interested me because earlier I had read reports by western
journalists who must have picked up the same story, probably
from the same source. (One had even written of 'the scream of
jet bombers' over her own head.) So how could I blame Spiderman for his credulity?

Meantime he began to ask me how the British had survived
German bombing in the last war. Did everyone in London

have their own shelter, and live in it? No? Then what had people done, at least while the raids lasted? Well, I said, most of us had gone on with whatever we were doing. Did the rich all have their own shelters today? No? And so on. I could see that he was finding most of my answers hard to believe, as well as deflationary, and I thought that he had probably seen one or more of the doomsday anti-nuclear propaganda films which have been so widely shown. He was genuinely afraid. He wanted me to be afraid too, and he hoped that in face of this new threat (perfectly real to him) I should begin to think of him and his horrible friends as protectors from something worse. But alongside his fear another feeling was visible, which woke sympathy. Half of his nature wanted the peril to be real and great. He longed to be tested and proved a hero. It was difficult not to warm a little to that.

In quite a different way that afternoon's conversation was a turning-point. The many questions and answers about wartime London must have been retailed to Kenyatta, and may have at last convinced him and Lobster-Eyes and the others that I might after all be the person I said I was. Up till then they had insisted on believing that my passport was a fake and that I pretended age and decrepitude as a cover for my real role as a secret agent. (Kenyatta accused me of this openly; Lobster-Eyes only laid elaborate traps designed to show it up.) I think they hoped that, failing any other proof of my guilt, this if it could be successfully foisted on me would prove the rest.

Kenyatta one day wound up an interrogation by giving me a packet of chocolates (I think part of the programme of alternating tough methods with soothing). The next time Spiderman came in I offered him one; and the same with the others. Fuzzy and Sambo were delighted, but Spiderman, though he accepted, was visibly not sure that he should. The next time he came in I asked him to take several for the little child whose voice I had heard at times outside in the hall. He seemed at first not to understand, then said I was mistaken: there was no child. When I insisted he said there was only 'small small baby' — whose wails too I had heard.

I gave up; but each time I ate a chocolate I made its foil wrapping paper into a boat — and it is a measure of how small an occupation is valuable to a prisoner, that I actually looked forward to making these, because of the time, little as it was, that they used up. When I had a fleet of five I asked Spiderman to give them to the child. He took them without demur, but as he left the room I saw him crumple them up in his hand. A week or more later Fuzzy was letting me out to go to the washroom when I heard a ripple of giggles, and had a glimpse just before they disappeared of Spiderman playing with a little girl of six or seven. Perhaps it was not so much that I was not allowed to know of this child's presence, as that she was not allowed to know of mine.


'We are ready to risk everything, even our lives, for the Cause,' Spiderman declaimed one day, lounging in an armchair which had been carried into my room for the use of an interrogator, and playing with his AK47 while he ate chocolates. He was genuinely offended when I said it seemed to me that he was not risking his life, only mine and other people's. That was the nearest I ever came to sharp words with any of them. I made it a rule never to raise my voice or show anger or resentment, and never to treat any of them with other than the most scrupulous politeness. This was partly from self-interest: for my own survival I needed good behaviour from them, and I could hardly expect it if I did not give it. But much more, I kept it up because it pleased me to treat them with courtesy. Rudeness or boorishness would have been a lowering of standards, thereby giving in to them. The keeping up of his own standards is of prime importance to a prisoner: it is the only thing under his own control. And it is natural, when you know that you may be near your end, to want to do your best.

There were never less than two, nearly always four, armed

men outside my door, and as I came and went between my room and the washroom I never once saw any of them doing anything. They lounged and giggled and arranged their hair, ate chocolates, played with their weapons, stared into space. 'My God,' I thought one day, 'they are leading drearier lives than I am.'

After a time I learned to vary the reciting of vocabularies with a kind of game, picking some easy word and counting as many similar words in as many languages as I could. To have stuck to synonyms would have been too restrictive: I counted words expressing the same ideas as my key-word. Thus I could make a great wheel from each beginning, and extend it to last a long time. The game needed discipline, or the shape of the wheel would have been lost.

I believe that I chose the key-words at random, but presently I noticed that they were all on a theme: light, liberty, love, air, to run, sunrise or daybreak, and the like. Never mind: they gave real pleasure. I would recommend this occupation to any hostage; it is very good practice for languages and for keeping the mind working. But you would know that it was time to change to something else if the key-words began to turn dark.

I often thought that I could get rid of time by making up crossword puzzles or doing anagrams or something similar, but instinct recoiled. It is not being physically a prisoner that hurts, but being unable to do anything that has a meaning outside. If I had ever learned to pray or to meditate, imprisonment would have been time gained for me, not time lost.

By now I had been a prisoner for three weeks or more, and still no one had tired of looking for clues in my address-book. At home I had begun numbering the pages, but had not gone far. One day Kenyatta said, suddenly alert: 'Page 5 is missing.'

I had chewed it up some while before. But by the grace of God I caught sight of the other half of the sheet, now unattached, lying askew further forward in the book. 'No, here it is,' I said, pulling it out for him. It was blank; otherwise he would have seen that it did not follow page 4 alphabetically.

'There's no number on it,' he said, not wholly fooled.

'No, because there are no names on it either. If I'd filled one in I'd probably have filled in the page number too. The Bs start on page 7.' And so they did. Twenty seconds or so passed very slowly. Then he began to turn the pages again.

Another time Kenyatta and Lobster-Eyes stopped at a name with a military rank attached, and the words 'Chelsea Barracks' written after it.

'Who is this?' Lobster-Eyes asked.

'An old friend.'

'Why "Chelsea Barracks"?'

'The Irish Guards' Officers' Mess is there.'

'You are lying.'

'As you like.'

Kenyatta cut in. 'There's no need to waste time. Chelsea Barracks is the headquarters of the SAS.'

'Is it? I wouldn't know.' I was interested that he should know or think this.

For some days afterwards Lobster-Eyes remained convinced that I must actually be a member of the SAS myself — which made me wonder what on earth he could think it is. The idea never wholly left them that I must be in some way connected with it, and in the following weeks many hours of fruitless cross-questioning were spent on trying to learn facts about it from me. One day to keep them occupied, and diverted from potentially more dangerous subjects, I told them that I had slightly known the founder of the SAS long ago. I was at once ordered to write down everything I knew about him. This was a bonus since it occupied time. I wrote them reams about his dead brother (but without mentioning the death), and a long, laudatory and patriotic account of the formation of the SAS in

135

1941, but nothing more recent. I was interested to find that none of them had ever heard of the German parachute invasion of Crete; for some time they actually thought that I must be talking of some quite recent operation, and certainly they had no idea where Crete is. Nor had they ever thought of the SAS as parachutists.

Then they wanted to know who else I knew in the regiment. I gave them a selective biography of one of its original members, admitting that he had been one of my greatest friends. Where was he now? What was he doing? I said I had no idea. Why not? I had not heard from him for some years. Why not? He had gone to Scotland, I said. I did not add that he had gone in a box with brass handles, to join his forefathers there.

This game provided light relief at the time, but it was not wise. It broke a basic rule: never give interrogators any information whatever, no matter how harmless, if it is not necessary to. For you cannot foresee what use they may put it to, what it may be distorted into, or whether you may need to say something later which it contradicts.

To write myself as far as Megara had taken me several days, working as slowly as I could make myself go, because I did not know whether or not I should be allowed more paper when I ran out, and because I did not know how long I might have to make this game last. By the time I had written myself into Epirus and back another week had gone by, and I was beginning to think that Dante got one thing wrong. To recall felicity *nella miseria* is not the sharpest of pains, it is sweet water to drink in the desert. Spiderman brought another exercise-book and I went on filling my time by filling it.

I am no city dweller: that must be obvious, since everything I have remembered and written down so far has been about remote country. But in this century it is hard to avoid spending at least some time in cities, and I had to do my share. Athens when I first went there had only a few hundred thousand people in it; there was five miles of fairly open country between the city and the Piraeus. Kolonaki was still a maze of early-nineteenth-century houses, behind their date in style, so that many were eighteenth-century in flavour, roofed with cockled red clay tiles and finished by a line of acroteria all the way along the lowest course, to stop the wind getting under and ripping them off. The streets were down-at-heel but clean, smelling of pine trees and lantana in the summer, and pine trees and roasting chestnuts in the winter. There were stalls selling hot, quoit-shaped bread stuck all over with sesame seeds, and corn-cobs being turned over charcoal in Stadium Street. Aeolou Street was a joy to the eye, with the Parthenon floating ethereally at its end, and along it the tall houses of the dead-and-gone sea-captains and the little houses and shops of the bellows-makers sandwiched in between. Modern change was of course already under way. A friend who had a house at the foot of Mount Lycabettus had pulled it down, built a block of flats on the site, and lived in the top one himself. He was about thirty; he said that in his childhood the street behind the house had been virtually a country road and he could remember waking in the mornings to the sound of the milk-carts rumbling in to the city.

Outside of two or three main hotels, no restaurant or taverna served a complete meal. You went to certain places to eat meat, to others for pastries, others for dishes made with milk products, and so on, just as you buy different things in different shops. This gave me a particular pleasure. I had often pestered nannies and governesses for a reason why a meal should be eaten in a fixed order, and always been given the same unsatisfactory answers, that 'it wouldn't be good' in a different order, or 'because that's the proper way'. It seemed characteristic of the Greek love of freedom, even if in a rather minor detail, that you could eat a meal in any order you liked.

Streetlights were few and feeble, and in the houses — mostly behind wooden shutters — their light was feebler still. At night the city twinkled like a colony of glow-worms, a lovely sight to look down on from the mountains.

Ramshackle trams ran along the three or four main streets. I believe they had been bought for a song in 1946 from Liverpool Council, which had declared them defunct, but they clanged round Athens at a fair clip with passengers clustered on them like bees in a swarm. There were few private cars about, partly because Greece had no money for imports but also because a government at its wits' end to devise tax laws that Greeks could not all evade had laid down simply that anyone who owned a car should have his income tax doubled. This cut down car-ownership dramatically, so it did not bring in very much revenue, but it greatly increased the use of taxis and thus gave livelihoods to a lot of drivers. There was an endearing snobbery in the upper ranks of Athenian society about the choice of a taxi. Not the smart or new or comfortable-looking ones, for they might belong to any contemporary go-getter; the thing was to choose the oldest, most broken-down wagon still supporting an engine that you could see. And why? Because these resuscitated wrecks dated from before the war, their owners had almost certainly fought in it, and probably they had taken the vehicle apart and buried it piecemeal to make sure that it did not fall into enemy hands. These were the men — and their families — that needed custom loyal to them, against up-and-coming entrepreneurs. Paul Melas of blessed memory knew many of them by name.

I cannot tell what the new rich who have taken over today's concrete Athens may be like; but the old guard then had brought their country through the valley of the shadow because they were close to it and because they had faith. The end of the war had brought a new order of existence in on

138

them, but it had not swamped them yet. Their customs had changed, but in ways which none could criticize. At their lunch parties only one course would be served, with bread and fruit to fill the corners. In these houses it had been customary in the past to cook enough food each day for a number of extra guests — not because they were expected but because they might arrive by chance and one must be ready in case they did. But if no one came the food was not wasted. Each big house kept an open kitchen door to a chosen few of the needy. These were not condescended to or pauperized in any way, and did not imagine that they were; only if they wanted a square meal any day, they knew where to get it. In the year or two after the war, when food and money were both still very scarce, few households could keep the custom going, but as many as could manage it, did. Today it is unheard of, and would probably be condemned as capitalist bullying or a relic of feudalism. I can only say that in practice it was good, for givers, receivers, and beholders.

Occasionally I dined in American households, where we drank whisky, and later many dishes were brought to table, made very handsomely from the best of imported canned foods. It was not taking anything from the mouths of starving Greeks (and many of them still were hungry) because it was all brought from the PX. Yet it was hard not to think it might have been better to live a shade less well, and buy at least fruit and vegetables from those who needed to sell them, and to have some contact, however little, with the people of the country. But these things can be easier said than done. A charming young American couple tried their hardest with fresh fruit and vegetables from the market, and thought them the best they had ever tasted. But they had to give it up. 'It made us sick to our stomachs,' they said unhappily. Not that they had not washed it all in permanganate crystals and so on. But their stomachs had not learned to accept food that had not come out of a can. It reminded me of Neil Gunn's wartime fable in which a whole population is held in slavery to a dictator because he has conditioned them till they cannot eat anything but the National Porridge which his government provides.

I do not know whether Greece is a democracy today or not; but if I have seen the democratic idea operating anywhere it was in Greece in the early 1950s. Elections were not rigged (or no party had a monopoly of the means of rigging), no man, however poor or ignorant, was afraid to speak his mind, or refrained from doing so, and the actual centres of power were still so small that men misusing it for political or personal ends were quickly identified and pulled down. This is not to say that chicanery and corruption did not exist: no doubt they did. But not on a crippling scale; and the culprits were exposed and sent packing often enough to keep the disease under control. Above all, the general feeling of the public at large was that they had suffered more than enough at the hands first of the Nazis, then of the Communists; now they needed nothing but a competent administration and their heads and hands free to put their own lives together again. And that is what they did.

Shadows of darker days could still fall across a street; but not often. I remember once walking away from a friend's house beyond the Ilissos river (the district has been flattened and rebuilt since) when a battered Land Rover came up from behind me. The driver did not go past, but cruised alongside me for a hundred yards or so; then he called out, asking if he could give me a lift. I did not answer. A desperate note came into his voice, totally unlike the note of hope or ingratiation normal to attempted pick-ups. 'I'll take you anywhere you like,' he said, 'and put you down the moment you tell me. But *please* get in.' I looked at him. He was thirty-five or forty. The vehicle might be his own, but they were rare in Athens; more likely it belonged to a contractor. The look on his face was of utter fear. I said: 'I'm going to Constitution Square,' thinking that he did not look likely to be going that way himself.

'I'll take you there.' He had already got the passenger-door

140

open. I had to walk round to get in, and got a glimpse as I did so of a big box strapped to the floor, with a sack over it. He moved off at once in the right direction, at a speed that would draw no attention. We came up to a main crossing with a roundabout. A police car appeared suddenly in front of us, blocking our traffic-lane. As we entered the roundabout, another pulled out from a turning and boxed us in. They would have had twice the Land Rover's speed: its driver had no chance of breaking away and did not try to, but docilely drew in to the kerb and got out. So did I. Two of the four policemen came up to us and he proffered a pack of documents which they hardly bothered to look at. I offered mine.

'Who is this?' they asked him, taking it for granted that I should know no Greek.

'I don't know, I've never seen her before. I was giving her a lift to Constitution Square.' I started to say something to confirm this, but he signed to me not to. One of the policemen said something to him which I did not understand, and he answered, 'As you like.' I looked at him. There is a moment we must all know, of realization that absolute disaster is about to fall: in that moment we lose the desperate desire to avert it and instead are swept by a blind urge to pull it on ourselves. Every line of his face and body told that he was at that point. He said to me: 'You'd better go away. I'm sorry.'

One of the policemen walked round to the back of the truck, turned up the canvas hood, leaned in and jerked the sack away. 'Open up,' he said. The driver handed him a key. 'There's nothing you can do,' he said to me. 'Please go now.' The policeman nodded my dismissal and I walked away up the street. From the end of it I looked back. They were still standing there. Smuggler? Civil-war fugitive on the run? Common criminal? Not that, I think, but I shall never know.


Athens today means retsina to millions. It is widely thought

of now as the national drink of Greece, and gets bottled and
exported on a surprisingly large scale considering how few
people actually like it. But it properly belongs only to Attica
and one or two other districts. Most of the country has always
made and still does make its wine as others do. The flavour of
retsina comes from caulking the barrels with pine resin, perhaps
originally as a preservative. The custom is certainly old: there
is what seems like a reference to it in Virgil. But Greek wines
used not to be standardized; every farmer or small proprietor
made his own, so that it was never the same in any two places
or any two years, and it was this that prevented an export
trade from building up. Buyers tend to want to know what
they will get next time.

In Greece it is usual to take your own bottle to any grower
or supplier to be filled. When I was first there half a litre cost
about twopence-halfpenny. When I left, a demijohn was about
five shillings. The tavernas still have their rows of huge barrels
and draw the wine off in tin or copper pots with handles, to
serve to customers. These tins used to hold an oke (an old
Turkish measure, about 450 drams), a half-oke, and a quarter
or 'katostariko. Greece has gone metric since, and the oke has
been abolished. For nostalgia's sake the quarter-litre pot has
been named *mikroutsiko*, but it sounds false, and I think only
rubs salt into the wound.

At first I was not taken with Greek wines. But if one is to
enjoy a country fully one must get a taste for its proper drinks,
and the learning did not take long. It is no use to compare
Greek wines with those of, say, western Europe: they are not
the same kind of drink nor meant for the same circumstances.
Retsina is delicious drunk under its native sun, always with
food to go with it, pungent dishes prepared with olive oil,
garlic, herbs, goat's cheese and the like; and at sunset on a
seashore, with slivers of cucumber, and olives and fishes' eggs
and rings of octopus. (The Greeks hold rightly that you should
never drink without eating.) And it is a delight to drink it at
certain places and times in England, for the thoughts and com-

pany it conjures up. To each pleasure its own natural place and honour.

A problem beset me in writing down these last recollections. My interrogators jumped to the conclusion that I must have been working in Greece for British Intelligence. Why else should I have been there at all, let alone learned the language? I could see that they were never going to believe the truth: that I had gone there entirely on my own, on a total capital of £68 and a return ticket, because from the age of about eight onwards it was the country that above all others I wanted to see. I had taken what jobs I could find, and luck had been very good to me, throwing me amongst strangers who saw what the passion was that possessed me — the passion to fit dream and reality into each other like mortice and tenon — and helped me on my way, finding me jobs and giving me friendship. None of that would have made any sense to my captors, born free, yet slaves to politics and propaganda as they were, fancying themselves 'freedom-fighters' without having ever had an inkling of what freedom is.

They did not of course read all that I wrote; did not even attempt to. Only Kenyatta had good enough English, and he had other responsibilities. But now and then they read a passage at random, and this made me very cautious about what I wrote. One of my jobs had been with the British Naval Mission. That would have spelled nothing less than James Bond to them, and would have cooked my goose for me. So I put in vague phrases that would give no clue if they were read, and made marks in the margin to remind myself to clarify them if or when I was free again and still had the text.

Kenyatta and the others came back again and again, in their questionings, to what my work in Athens had been. But luckily men who enjoy the flavour of their own cleverness often answer their own questions. Kenyatta already knew that I had worked for the Red Cross in Cyprus; he eventually (and wrongly) drew the conclusion that I had done so in Greece too, and confronted me with it as a fact instead of asking. If he had asked I should have told him his mistake: I lied whenever I thought it necessary but had found myself sticking in face of that one. However, once he had put the idea into his own head I thought I had no duty to disabuse him. It is on such small errors and unreasoned scruples that our lives hang once we have fallen among the apes, outside law and order.


Among the scraps of paper at the bottom of my handbag was a household shopping-list: beef, cheese, cauliflower, and the like. Lobster-eyes read it again and again without managing to make anything sinister of it. But when he turned it over he saw a telephone message that had been jotted down on the back: 'Dinner Walter, Sunday, 8 o'clock.' Suspicion shimmered off him almost like the spray from a fountain.

'Who is Walter?'

'An old friend.'

'Where is he?'

'In Cornwall. He lives near us.'

'Do-on't lie to us. We know him.'

'I'm afraid you don't.'

'We know him very well. He is *beeg* man.'

'No. About average size, I should say.'

His face twisted with fury. 'He is big *military* man. We know everything about him.'

Walter had of course fought the last war; but he has been a civilian for very many years now, and I said so. It was no good. The eyes narrowed, showing that cunning was being exercised.

'What is his job?'

'He's retired. But he's a very fine gardener.'

'Don't lie. We know.'

If Schiller had ever had to do with terrorists no one could

144

have grudged him his dictum: 'Against stupidity the gods themselves struggle in vain.'

Life may play us unkind tricks but it often turns them to our very great pleasure and good. Once in the late 1960s I came to Greece alone, angry, smarting under much busybodying and some injustice, oppressed by clouds presaging more of the same thing, and very much hurt. I therefore found it necessary to do something difficult and at least potentially risky, merely as an ointment to put on raw feelings.

The fact that we wanted to buy a house in some lonely spot gave me a starting point. I picked from the map a length of coast so inaccessible and barren that I could meet nobody who had actually been along it, and decided to walk it, keeping within sight of the sea all the way. From road-head to road-head I reckoned this should take four days. Even I could see that I was not likely to find a suitable house along the route, or even land to build one on, for that would need communications of some kind. But I had hopes for something near to one end or the other of it. And I was alone and on my way: therefore something worthwhile would turn up.

I walked in a morning clarity that washed away preoccupations as sunrise washes out candle-light. When I was tired and hot enough I swam, in a lovely solitude, shadeless as a heliograph, diving naked from the rocks into two or three fathoms of water flecked with little round, dark fishes. As I walked on the hours shimmered away easily enough, and life became once more very good.

'Anchored' ('made fast') Greece is what the Greeks call the mainland north of the Gulf of Corinth — as if the Peloponnese were only holding station and might up sails and off into the sunrise any morning.

As I got near to the tip of the headland (looking back I

could count nine spurs behind me) I saw that I should have to leave the water's edge and climb over the saddle. I was thirsty. The heat was terrific and sweat poured in streams off me. I had eaten a couple of mouthfuls of cheese, but when water is short food is not much help. It was a very steep climb, and all this ground was treeless, though thickly and hamperingly covered with prickly *pournari* scrub and low-growing, long-spined wild olive. After a time I could hardly keep putting one foot in front of another. After each spurt I scanned the glaring tilt of rocks for the next bush tall enough to throw a splash of shade, made for it, and collapsed until the blood picked up its rhythm again. At first I covered a couple of hundred yards at a time, but the distance kept shortening, so that I had to do with poorer and poorer shade, and once simply fell face-down among the thorns and sprawled there until I could get up again. At last, about five hundred feet up, I reached the first pine trees, lay full-length under one, and got on better after that.

There were dozens of tiny tracks up here, made by resin-tappers going from one tree to another. All the trees had been broached and bore tins tied with string round their trunks to catch the gum.

I misjudged my route and instead of crossing the saddle where the headland was lowest I struck the crest at its highest point, where a palisade of rocks stood straight on end like great silver faggots. I climbed painfully round and between these. From my feet the hill dropped away almost like a cliff, then levelled out into a slope dotted with pines and, lower down, with olives. To seaward it ran out into a little, rounded, fertile peninsula. Straight below me lay a bay with a grey shingle shore, trees, a small white church and a few houses.

I climbed down as quickly as I could, coming out on to a low ridge which ran just below the church. There was a little gate on which a notice asked that one see it well closed, and beyond that a green wooden door. Once inside the church I could stand no longer but sank to my knees and then almost to prostration – and it occurred to me that though this might look more pious than it was, at least it would not look irreverent. Not that there was anyone to see, but I hate to do things which give offence even if I am not known to be doing them.

The cool flagstones and the blessed gloom revived me, and the church had handsome frescoes of the royal saints, Constantine and Helena, as well as of the patron of the place, St Basil. I lit a candle and presently went down to the houses on the shore.

A young man came to meet me and led me down small cascades of whitewashed steps on to a stone-built platform with a roof of leaves. There was a hut adjoining it, and deep water at its feet. Under the leaves were the usual little square tables and rush-bottomed chairs, and a great pail of fresh water, its sides still cool and streaming from the well. A family party was gathered there: parents, uncle, nephews and grown sons. An older man came, carrying in a cloth a cold cooked fowl which he began to dismember. When it was in pieces several tables were put together and we feasted.

A party of strangers meantime had been gathering at the taverna in the throat of the bay, where a motorable track spilled out of the hills from the other shore. One of the new arrivals came to inspect us: he was the captain of the military district. He talked for a few minutes, not without pomposity, asked me one or two questions in fair English, then said he would swim. He went into the hut and emerged some time later in bathing-trunks and his military hat. When he had swum away in it the mother of the family said he was after all a good man, and looked after the district well.

A discussion now arose about whether or not any but the Orthodox were truly Christians. The mother of the family held that Catholics, Protestants and the like were not so, although baptized. Their priests had not the Apostolic Succession, so they could not be real Christians. Then she took a quick turn through the Double Procession of the Paraclete. Her eldest son argued for the reunion of the Churches, but the notion scandalized her on other grounds besides the provenance of the Holy Spirit. The last and most determinedly held was the difference in Easter dates. 'But after all,' her son said, 'it was a very long time ago, Mother. Nobody can really say *exactly* when it happened.'

'Anathema!' the old lady brought out, raising both hands above her head in a hieratic gesture of condemnation. 'That I should live to hear my own son say that I don't know what day my Saviour rose on!'

I thought that if I were a visitor from nowhere and had walked over the cliffs to some lonely Cornish fishing-cove, these would not be the problems and passions I should hear being thrashed out.

Two of the men were going out that evening to lay nets in the bay. They set off an hour before sunset, taking me with them to land me on the next headland, whence I could walk on to the village of Aliki. The wind roughened up, but after warm and vinous farewells and pressing offers of food for the journey we pushed off. 'It'll be all right,' Vangeli said when we were well out into the bay, 'it's calmer here.' The boat was bucking like a horse, the bow dropping five feet at a time. He pointed up to the top of the grey cliff facing us. 'You see the single pine tree?' It stood dark and fluffy against a white, angry sky. 'You must climb up to that. On the other side of it there are some winter sheepfolds, and from them you'll find the path down to Aliki.'

The rocks inshore were jagged and unfriendly-looking: it seemed mad to try to bring the boat close in. But: 'We'll try it,' Vangeli said cheerfully. 'Can you jump?' And jump I did, without trouble, so close and so steady did he hold her for the few seconds needed. Then it was a steep climb, but the landmarks were all as he had said and the path good when I reached it. By now the sun was going down, the sky darkening and colouring richly behind storm-clouds, the Halcyon Sea (for that was what now lay before me) a ruffled red-gold. Behind me the many inlets and capes of the Gulf of Geraneia fell away. In front the headland reached out into the sunset and ended in a mighty bluff, cut off sheer. Beyond the saddle of this gleamed the waters of the next inlet, gold now; still further on, a chain of islets lay coal-black on the brilliant water. Behind these again the mountains of Roumeli receded, hazy and darkening, the whole view dominated — glorified — by the huge bulk of Mount Helicon, so near and vast and steep that I could only just believe in it.

Vangeli had mentioned a chapel of the Holy Virgin, beside which there was a spring. I found and drank from it, then climbed the rocks to a cave screened by boulders and bushes, and on the little, flat, grassy space in front of it in the fast-darkening air I settled for the night.

In the morning I walked down past the ruins of a little Venetian castle into Aliki: a lovely place, but disfigured by the shacks and tents of summer visitors. The first of these whom I passed insisted upon giving me hot cocoa; he came from the Piraeus, she from the village of Domvraina not far away. They said that they came here every summer, and that the water was exceptionally heath-giving: it made everything inside you run like water. But I had been wrong to drink from the spring by the chapel. Not only did it lack this virtue, it had harmful worms in it.

Excessive kindness now diverted me from my plan to stick to the coast. A road-head of a sort reached Aliki; and a hatted, spectacled young medical student insisted that I come with her, sharing the passenger-seat of a lorry, to Thisbe. (I went partly for the sake of the name.) She hoped in the autumn to come to London; meantime she plied me with peaches and arranged for me to go on by bus to the village of Hostia, at the root of a long peninsula called on my map 'the Holy Ones'. Everyone insisted that to walk round the Holy Ones was quite impossible. But a father and his three sons were going down with a lorry to Sarandi, some way along it, and I went with them.

At the head of the inlet north of the Holy Ones the map showed a village called Zaltsa. But everyone in Sarandi stuck

149

to it that I could not get there round the coast. There were no paths, because no one ever went; and no one ever went because there was no water. Two men together would be able to do it, carrying enough for themselves (it would take two to three days), but only in the cool weather. If I were to try it now, and alone, I should die on the way. 'We should hear presently from Zaltsa,' someone said, 'that you hadn't arrived there. News travels, even in places like this. And we'd take a boat out to look for you. But it would be too late by the time we found you.' Then they said that I could get to Zaltsa through the hills, going back over the neck of the peninsula, crossing a saddle and putting up for a night at the monastery of St Seraphim.

All this time I was thinking that ordinary people often manage to cross great tracts of the Sahara or the Gobi without dying, so a small stretch of Greek coast could not be lethal. But I must explain that what I was doing was even stupider than it may sound so far. I had read a book by that remarkable Frenchman Professor Bombard, who devised a plan by following which no shipwrecked sailor need ever die of thirst in an open boat. Its basis was that a man can survive on sea-water for up to ten days without doing himself real damage, if he follows certain basic rules; and that within ten days anywhere far out at sea it will have rained. The rules were roughly that he must drink about half a litre of sea-water per day, not more or less; that in hot conditions he must keep wetting his body with sea-water to counteract evaporation; and that he must exert himself as little as possible. After twenty-five years working in the Oceanographical Museum of Monte Carlo on this theory, Professor Bombard tested it on himself, and succeeded in crossing from the Canaries to Bermuda in a rubber dinghy, catching plankton and squeezing flying-fish for survival. It took him, I think, three months.

I was immensely impressed by this feat, and now concluded that just a few days of sea-water would be child's play. I clean forgot that the intrepid professor's first attempt had been at crossing the Mediterranean from north to south; it had been a total failure, and he had been rescued by the Royal Navy only just in time. Afterwards he had realized the reason: the salinity of the Mediterranean is much higher than in less enclosed waters. And the salinity of the Gulf of Corinth is of course higher than elsewhere in the Mediterranean.

I set off from Sarandi with a hunk of bread, two tomatoes, and a pint of water; with directions to get to St Seraphim, and largely intending to do so, yet with that rough-edged, taut strip of my mind which does not respond to reason drumming a different tune. There was no real conflict. With my head full of the joy of travel and the splendour of Helicon I reached a place where an infinitesimal goat-path seemed to divide. I had been told there was a point where I must bear right: the appearance of a left-hand path was delusory. Was this it? Surely not: the right-hand track was even fainter than the other. I turned left and committed myself to the Holy Ones without really acknowledging that I had done so.

When darkness fell I found a few feet of fairly level ground, unrolled my thin sleeping-bag (I possessed one by now) beside a cypress bush, ate a little bread and a tomato, drank a few mouthfuls of my fresh water, and went to sleep under the slimmest and finest of new moons sliding behind the crest of the mountain. Far down the recession of headlands towards Geraneia an occasional lamp gleamed gold. Sage and cistus were strong in my nostrils. Before me across the Gulf, the villages along the northern shore of the Peloponnese hung like star-cities in the blackness of the sky.

In the morning I could see encouragingly close above me the castle-like crest of the ridge. Only cross this, and either the monastery or the sea would appear. I crossed it, and all that appeared was another crest, higher and longer, and cut off from me by a ravine which I must find a way round. But this is the most ordinary of disappointments in mountain walking. It did not take too long. By now it was becoming clear that there was no falling-away of ground towards the north, instead

151

a tilt to westward was beginning as one ridge succeeded another. There was no mistaking now that I was on my way to the Holy Ones.

I thought I had better make the best speed I could while the cool of the morning lasted — partly because I had lost my battered hat the night before. When I had sweated over a great many ridges I got a sight of the sea at last at the tip of the promontory. But the spur I was on ended in a raw cliff, and I had to go down four hundred feet and up the other side before I could get to the last headland.

The journey back along the northern cliffs of the promontory was still rougher going, with the sharp limestone chopped into great furrows and bearing nothing better than prickly scrub. So I was delighted when I saw a small cove not too far out of reach. I climbed down and on the shore found a two-roomed white house, closed and deserted. Inside, through a dusty broken window, I could see the usual clean, simple peasant furnishings and, astonishingly, a gleaming perambulator. It must have been brought there by boat, and there was nowhere it could have been wheeled except up and down the mud floor of the house.

I swam, and drank my ration of sea-water. It did not lessen the feeling of thirst at all, but I reminded myself that it must at least do something to replace the salt and the water I had sweated out on the way.

A black dog looked suddenly round the clay bake-oven at me, barked uncertainly, and ran away among the rocks. Its presence spoke the presence of humans: and so perhaps did a big fish-spear lying in front of the house. But there was no one there, and the spear was rusty. I drank a few drops more from my water bottle. The liquid was hot and flat, and it washed away the taste of salt for only a few minutes. I found a cracked cistern, uncapped: the dog kept circling round and round it. But there was no water there. The dog would die,

152

but he seemed already mad. Even so he would not come with me. Before leaving I soaked my bathing-suit and wore it like a scarf on my head. No doubt I must have seemed mad too, if there had been anyone to judge, but the wet coolness of it was wonderful.

Up on the cliff again it was difficult to keep going in the wilderness of sharp rocks and scrub and the vertiginous, shimmering glare, but at last I turned the point of a headland and saw two or three hundred feet below me the most perfect little cove the eyes could rest on. As I made towards it along the cliff edge I saw that it lay at the mouth of a narrow, very long ravine. To reach the head of the ravine could take an hour or more. But facing me on the opposite cliff, a few yards out from the shore, a green streak on the rock showed where fresh water must run down into the sea. Caution died. The cliff offered a network of fissures and outhanging, salt-silvered cypress roots as tough and twisted as ropes. I scrambled and swung and zigzagged down to the shore, which was made entirely of pink-and-white pebbles, very pale, but ground at the far side, perhaps from the friction of some current, to coarse sand of a slightly deeper colour than the rest. The water was of the most intense blue-green that I had ever seen.

I stripped and plunged in and swam across to where the lime-green trace of the spring showed. The minuscule mosses were vivid on the stone and as dry as velvet. But the coolness of the water in the bay, the soft ripple of it along my limbs after the hardness of the rock and thorns, and the darkness to the eyes looking down into it after the dazzle above felt as Paradise must, drowning and drawing away the disappointment. I drank the sea, and dived, and drifted, and longed to stay suspended there for ever.

When I landed at last I drank another mouthful or two of my fresh water, ate the last tomato, and stretched out full-length in the narrow strip of shade at the cliff foot: shade that of itself filled the mind with gratitude. But soon I felt a kind of unease, and I began to look for how I should get out of this place again. I saw that just inshore of the green streak a way could be found up the cliff: it looked as though goats might have used it sometimes, and it ended – or started – on a big flat rock that stood up two or three feet out of the water, a few yards from the shore. I felt a great lassitude, but got up to look more carefully at it. I had not gone two steps before I was seized with a spasm like the onset of dysentery.

I shall not go into details of the next few hours. Presently I could no longer get up, but only roll over a foot or two and then roll back on to a clean patch of sand. It came to me quite clearly that at last I had pushed my luck too far – it had been bound to happen one day – and I might well not get out of this. The villagers at Sarandi had been right. It seemed an odd way to go, neither foreseeable nor foreseen. Still, there was nothing I could do about it: no way of summoning help nor anyone to be summoned, nor duty to be fulfilled. I would concentrate simply on the physical onslaught.

Time went by, and as the heat began to drain out of the day, I began to put two and two together. I slowly realized that I was not actually getting worse. Logically therefore I must be going to get better. I was not suffering from dysentery, merely from stupidity: misapplication of Professor Bombard's theory about sea-water.

I saw that if I could get to the nearest human habitation all would be well. And I knew from the map that by now I must be within a mile or two of Zaltsa. If I could crawl up the cliff, will-power would probably get me the rest of the way; and I had better tackle it before dark. In another half-hour I managed to get on to my feet, holding my rucksack (it felt like a load of lead), and staggered into the sea. To get on to the flat rock took an age. The water first carried part of my weight, then sucked and clawed me back as soon as I tried to pull myself up from it. A last spasm nearly did for me before I landed sprawling face-downwards on the hot roughness of the rock, which was queerly reviving. Then I put on my clothes again and got going. From here on it was just a matter of little by little: yard by yard, rock by rock, till I reached first the cliff-top, then the crest of the headland. At last in the fading light that rests the eyes after sunset a wide gulf lay below me, with a great sweep of grey shingle shore. At first there seemed to be no habitation, and my heart sank. Then I saw three small stone houses against the cliff at the far side of the bay, nearly a mile away still. But as I went forward three or four neat huts of reeds and branches came into view on the shore, with a thin cooking-smoke going up from behind one of them, and two or three chairs standing out under a canopy of leaves. Civilization; humanity; the Ritz, no less.

I thought that I should like to put as good a face on things as possible, so when I got near I stopped and combed my hair and tidied myself up as far as I could. Then I walked towards the first hut, willing my legs to keep steady under me and trying to look as if I were out for a casual evening stroll. I could not have kept it up for more than a hundred yards or so, but I did not have to. A young woman appeared, leading a goat. She stopped and stared in astonishment, then greeted me in a strange language – which astonished me in my turn. But the mystified 'Whence comest?' which she finally produced showed that she had at least some Greek. She led me to a chair and gave me the ritual glass of water. She did not know it, but she was handing me life itself. Only when I had drunk four or five glassfuls without stopping did she ask how I had reached here. I told her that from Sarandi I had missed the way to St Seraphim and gone out to the end of the Holy Ones, and back along the coast. I could see that she thought it impossible.

While we talked, she had been preparing a treat for me without my knowing it. I had seen her fill a bucket with sea-water and put something into it. With all the pleasure that hospitality brings she now pressed on me a bottle of orange pop. At first I thought that I should not be able to get or keep it down, but I felt so desperately ill that nothing seemed to matter except the recognition of courtesy. I began to drink it, and its sugar revived me as I suppose nothing else could have.

By now the men were coming in from work, and they gathered round us. They too did not believe at first that I had been where I said; but when I had described to them the beach at the tip of the Holy Ones, the house on the shore and the black dog, and the blue-green cove, they knew it was all true.

The dog belonged to one of them. A couple of weeks ago he and his family had gone to that house by boat. The dog had seemed suddenly to become possessed: he had run off making strange noises and would let no one come near him. It was the same the next day: he would stare at them from a distance, but turn and run if they moved towards him. In the end they had had to leave him, reluctantly because they knew that once he had drunk the water in the cistern to below the level he could reach to (or it had evaporated, for they had left the cover off for him), he must die. 'It was as if he'd seen a nereid,' his owner said. To the Greek countryman the nereids, though they may be delightful, are deadly: a kind of water-witch.

As to the other cove, the part of my tale they found hardest to believe was that I had swum to where the green water-mark streaked the cliff. For it was known that that cove was unswimmable. Had I not noticed the extraordinary colour of the water in it? That was because it was bottomless, and the resulting current irresistibly sucked down any boat or swimmer. In the old days it used to be thought that the cause was a *gorgona* living there, but it was understood now that the immeasurable depth and the suction were the result of an earthquake. (I thought of Milton's 'dire chimeras and enchanted isles / And rifted rocks whose entrance leads to Hell'.) If I had stayed on the beach there, they said, I should certainly have died. They would have heard, perhaps tomorrow or in the next few days, from St Seraphim, that I had left Sarandi for the monastery but not reached it. They would have gone out to look for me by boat. But never would they have put into that cove; and crossing the mouth of it at a safe distance offshore one would not see a body lying on the strand, or

156

hear a hail, even if it were loud and strong. It was all very mystifying. I believe they sat up long that night discussing it. But I had reached my limit. A woman led me away into one of the huts, and I lapsed into sleep or semi-consciousness or both for a longish time.

The next day I found that I had stumbled on a very interesting little community. They were Albanians, and though the men spoke Greek the women talked a version of Albanian to each other and to their children. There were only about twenty souls here. Three families lived the year round in the three stone houses; they were fishermen. The rest were seasonal nomads. They spent most of the year, with others, 5,000 feet up on the flanks of Mount Helicon, herding goats or working the pine forests there. In summer they came down to St Seraphim and worked the vines and the olive groves belonging to the monastery, and these three or four families came down to the sea, built these huts, fished, and grew a few vegetables. They brought their drinking water here by donkey from a spring half a mile up the valley. Once a month someone took the fastest of their boats up the coast, a three-hour trip to Antikyra, east of Delphi; any little luxuries they needed they brought down from there. And at the end of the season the young men made a much longer foray, right round Cithaeron and Geraneia to the great city of Loutra, where they could blow in revelry most of what they had earned from the monks. They were astonished – and very interested – to learn that the sort of money they would spend in such a night would be enough to buy them a ticket to England.

Now what were the luxuries that, in a life of this kind, people would most desire? Sad to say, there were two transistor radios. But they were played only by the men, therefore only in the evenings; and they were not so jarring as they might have been, for the only station listened to kept up a continuous programme of Greek country songs, mostly with one voice and traditional instruments. There was a Petrogaz-driven stove, and a paraffin refrigerator stocked with fizzy drinks. The women did not allow themselves the luxury of these; but when the men wanted them, or a child had earned a treat, a bottle was brought out and warmed up in a bucket of sea-water (as my hostess had done for me the night before), since it would be dangerous to drink it cold. The men would buy a newspaper in Antikyra but they did not usually bring it back, because such things are of no use or interest to women. Finally there was great abundance of paper napkins stamped with the advertisement of a Greek brewer: a real luxury among people with no water supply and a passion for cleanliness. The whole place was as clean as a new pin. Not only did the women sweep the floors of their shacks ten feet above the tide-line and burn the little rubbish they made: they took brooms and swept the shingle in front of their doors.

The children naturally did not go to school, but they learned their religion and the Greek language and the three Rs from the monks in St Seraphim.

During the Greek revolts of the late eighteenth century and the War of Independence in the early nineteenth, both Greeks and Turks brought in Albanian mercenaries to help them, for the Albanians were recognized as more savage than either of the other races, and so each hoped to tip the scale with them. When the dust had finally settled, many of these imported cutthroats married Greek girls and settled too, in little colonies here and there. I ought to have known that there was one on Helicon.

One of the women had explained to me that the language they spoke to each other was Albanian, but her husband dismissed this as silly nonsense. 'We're Italians,' he said, 'or precisely, Sicilians.' I knew (because I had needed to know during the war) that the population of Sicily includes a two-fifths minority of people of Albanian blood, mostly claiming direct descent from the great sixteenth-century Albanian hero Scanderbeg. But it seemed remotely unlikely that they had any connection with the people of this inland shore, or that these people had ever heard of them. I was going to ask more when a grave, whiskered elder spoke up. 'No,' he said, 'we're not from Sicily. It was the Romans who brought us here. Fifteen hundred years ago, you know, the Romans held Greece. They brought the Albanians down with them as soldiers: that is, us.'

It recurred to me that a Roman general (Clodius Albinus? Septimius Severus?) had brought a Dacian legion down here. Not quite Albania, but unwritten history, slightly garbled, can stay vivid over very long reaches of time. Yet this had not the right ring about it. I asked whether they differed in blood from the Greeks of the area, or only in language. 'Ah, only language,' said the old man. 'The blood is the same.'

They went on to talk about events in the outside world, as Greeks always do; but they were not living in Byzantium like the matriarch of Ayios Basileos. They told me of the iniquities of the American war in Vietnam. They did not know where Vietnam was; several of them gave the distinct impression that it was somewhere on the other side of Mount Helicon, in the general direction of Thebes. But the phrases they used were familiar, out of conventional Communist Party literature.

I began to think about Antikyra. I had been there twice: it is a small and lovely natural harbour which for very many years has served an insignificant little bauxite mine. But in the early 1960s a NATO missile site was constructed in the mountain behind it. The road down to it was widened; some barbed-wire fencing appeared, and notices in Greek informed the few tourists who might make their way there that taking photographs was now forbidden. From then on a succession of Soviet freighters appeared in Antikyra harbour, loading bauxite. The men of Zaltsa said that whenever they went there now there was a Soviet ship tied up alongside, and they were always invited aboard and given a good time and brought up to date with world news. I asked what language this was done in. They said there were always one or two Greek-speakers among the crew, and this year there had been an Albanian-speaker as well. I thought this interesting, considering the hostility of

159

Albania towards the USSR as well as towards Greece. They told me it was the Soviet sailors who had first shown them how the monks of St Seraphim oppressed them, keeping them in miserable poverty and forcing them to work all the year for a pittance, in the name of childish superstitions. Life was not like that in the Soviet Union. The sailors brought down papers, too, written in Greek and telling the real truth about world affairs.

I felt very sad, for it was clear that the monastery was in fact completely supporting them. I let them talk on, and they began telling me that this part of Greece rightly belonged to them, and that one day there would be a National Liberation Struggle, and it would triumph, and the land would thenceforth belong not to the rich, brutal and superstitious monks but to themselves. Their talk had three main threads. The noble Russians, backed by the wise Harold Wilson, were doing everything in their power to stop the wicked and monstrous war in Vietnam. The ruthless Americans wished for this evil war because they were making money out of it; and though they were not physically at war with Greece they waged a savage economic war against her which was strangling the country. And finally, the western world except for Greece is made up of purblind Protestants and worse, Catholics. But 'the Russians are the same as us. They are Orthodox'. Reminded that Communists are atheists they fell into a brief, uneasy silence. They knew it to be true, but this new legend had tremendous attraction.

I remembered Patrick Leigh Fermor's account in *The Traveller's Tree* of the Rastafarians in Kingston, Jamaica. Compared with the hemp-dazed Dungle-men these goat-herds and fishermen were fit descendants of Pericles or Plato. But the processes of corruption, the insertion of the worm into the apple, were the same, and so, I thought, was the fantastic thoroughness with which the purveyors of this creed seek out and work upon any group they can reach, however small and seemingly unimportant.

I stayed three days in Zaltsa. By the end of the second I could drink goat's milk, kindly heated up and sugared for me by Maria (for so my hostess was called despite Albanian nationalism and Marxist anti-clericalism). It pained them all that I could not eat or drink anything else, for they killed a kid and held a feast in the stranger's honour; but that milk seemed more luxurious to me than anything they were eating did to them, and it was days before I could do much better.

They were reluctant to let me go before I was fitter. 'If you stayed a bit longer,' said the finest of the young men, speaking for the others as well as for himself, 'you could teach us to swim. You see, we know now that everybody in the rest of the world can swim. It makes us ashamed, that we can't. But no one here has ever done it. There's no one to show us how to begin.'

Before I left I did what I could to give them the idea, but I had not enough strength to stay long in the water, even in that warm sea, so I had to leave them to it. I would have spent longer there, but as I did not want a search-party turned out unnecessarily, I needed to get word back to Athens.

I have sometimes been asked why I wanted to do things of the kind I have been recalling. Why have I chosen acute discomfort, exhaustion, bad food, often no bed, no sanitation, sometimes mild danger, when these things were not necessary? The answer is that they were necessary in their own way: not for themselves but for the windows they open on the world. For most of our days we see only a very little of life; and it is not like we think it is. Do I know how it looks to an Eskimo or a Mexican? Of course not, and I cannot, unless I go and ask him. And there are few things more interesting to know, except how our lives look to God.

Then there is the pure excitement of breaking ground new to yourself (there is always someone to whom it is not new). Would Odysseus have been content in Ithaca, and grown a paunch, if he had sailed home with the rest of the fleet? Would that not have been a much harder fate for him than the one he was made to work out? Poseidon can have understood little about human nature. Only when Odysseus was loaded with new knowledge like a vine with grapes could he come home and tread it, and others ferment it and make it into wine for us all to drink ever afterwards.

For many years I thought it was the collection of knowledge that was all-important. I was wrong of course. Without knowledge we can understand nothing, therefore we hunt it. But intense as the pleasure of that may be, the collecting can hardly be important in itself, for if we do not convert what we gather into understanding, however inadequate, we might as well never go beyond the three Rs.

Now I am a prisoner, and may or may not emerge alive. That is the penalty of imprudently pursuing understanding. Was it worth it? Well, worth what? We lose nothing by death, because it changes the ground-rules of the game. Whatever we may lose, we shall not have to pay: dead debtors are out of reach by live duns. None the less, moral and emotional problems swell up. How can I justify the pain caused to those whom I love? I cannot at all. Yet, little as I understand about anything, the consequences so far of this hunt have hugely increased what glimmerings I had about more things than I went out to look for. So if I get back it will have been worth it, and if not, no one will be the worse.


Ayios Basileos and Zaltsa were two worlds geographically only a few miles apart, but revolving in their own isolated chapters of history as if centuries still divided them. And there were other places — to my mind the very best — where time made no boundaries at all. At the end of my first October in Greece an English friend took me to stay overnight with a shepherd family on Mount Parnassus. We were to go up before dawn the next morning with them, for they were bringing their flock down from the high pasture before the winter set in. John knew (and knows) Greece as well as anyone I have ever met, most Greeks included. He had spent time on Parnassus and knew the family well. They lived 600 feet above Delphi, in a large, low, sprawling house of absolute simplicity but absolute order. They were rich as shepherds go, with 350 head of ewes, and could have what they liked within reason. Also they had the high courtesy, so often found in inner Greece, of people conscious of an immensely long and honourable ancestry, even if it is a peasant one.

I am not much given to getting up before dawn, but there are places where it can be worth the pains of purgatory. The height and blackness of the sky that morning, the stars riding it like fishing-lamps, the silence and the great swell of the mountain looming up before us made the world feel whole and of one piece with the spirit — and so it pretty well was, up there.

The Greek shepherd or mountain man moves at a slow but very steady rate, not more than three miles an hour, and he halts every (guessed) half-hour for a breather, and perhaps a cigarette if he happens to have one, at alternate breathers. Distance is calculated by time, in cigarettes: not the time it takes to smoke them, but the number of such halts that will be made on the way. In height he does roughly a thousand feet an hour, up or down. This can be hard work if the going is very difficult, but it is not gruelling.

Dawn had reached the high pasture by the time we got there. A shepherd came down to meet us and told us that we had left things a day too long. A wolf had been down in the night and taken a hogget. This was an unlooked-for excitement and was discussed at length. Officially there were no wolves left on Parnassus, but here was proof of them. Many people were known to think that under the Germans the wolves had come back again. Heads were tilted gravely at the mention of that: it was passed as likely. The notion was that under a regime of human wolves the animal ones would naturally get

163.

a grip of the mountains again. At any rate, by the time it had all been discussed and the flock had been coaxed into the fold and milked and the brushwood put back across the entrance, every man on the upper slopes of the mountain had assembled to hunt the wolf; most with dogs, some with sticks and stones, and with the most astonishing random collection of firearms anyone could wish to see: old service rifles, rifles from the Balkan Wars, extraordinary shotguns (one of them clearly home-made, and the owner seemed to be cramming nails down the barrel); even a German service revolver. This merry crew went whooping and bounding through the silver-fir forest for hours, but without putting up the wolf. In the end, after knocking over one or two smaller creatures instead, they all regathered for lunch and then to start the count of the beasts. I was told to sleep while this went on; a few silver-fir branches were cut and piled on top of each other, and I was taught how, if you lay them all in the same direction and lie on them with your head towards the thicker ends, none of the needles will stick into you. It was perfectly true, and the springiness of the branches, swaying slightly under one, and the scent of them, gave more nearly the sensation that rooks must get in their nests than I ever expected to feel.

Just now as I was writing there came the sound of an explosion; a shot, then a vehicle with a siren, travelling fast; a nearer shot, and then one from this building. But the vehicle did not stop. Now there is silence, and I am securely locked in. It is a silence that has nothing in common with the tranquillity and freedom and armed rumpus and nearness to God of Parnassus; and it is strange, and yet natural, that a thread should run through so many chances from the one to the other.

By the time the flock had been allowed to graze and driven

down on to their winter pasture, and milked again and put in their right place, it was evening. When we reached the house lamps had been lit and John's attention was needed.

At this time nearly every Greek shepherd from his mother's knee to the grave lived in a suit of hand-knitted neck-to-wrists-to-ankles goat's-wool underclothing: champion protection against the winters, but how it could be borne in the summer is another question. Man is superbly adaptable. It had occurred to the family that a good income could be got from turning out these formidable garments faster than their women could knit them. (They took a year or more each.) So after consultation with an English visitor to Delphi they had written to Bradford for a catalogue, and chosen and ordered a knitting-machine. It cost over £400, a very respectable sum of money at that time. But they had got more than that put by, and had decided.

Here however the story diverges from one of business acumen into high fairy-tale. The machine was already paid for and on its way: they were expecting to collect it from Itea, the seaport below Delphi, in a week or so. But they had not sent only for a machine. They had stipulated that a skilled man must come with it, install it, and teach them how to use it. He was to stay for a month as their guest.

The thought of that man has haunted me ever since. What happened to him? He was about to walk through the Looking-Glass, but would the other side be paradise or torment for him? No one up here spoke English. And if, as I have always hoped, he adapted and found the life as simple and as complicated and as profoundly instructive as it was, how could he bear to go back? Or perhaps the pulls of home and work and so on would get him back all right; but how could he ever settle for Bradford life again? Or did he come back untouched, and down his pint and say it was a rum go, or whatever they say in Bradford, but he was bloody glad to be out of it? I shall never know. I have often wanted to write a story about him, but I lack the necessary knowledge and understanding. If anyone who knows his Bradford men and his knitting-machinery would like to take it up, I should love to read the result.

As I was beginning that last paragraph another rattle of small-arms fire broke out. Three hours and fifty-one minutes have passed since the earlier one. This time my hopes rose higher than ever before, for the sharp little spit of the Soviet rifles was followed by two ear-splitting crashes: a mortar being fired out of the compound of this house. I wished it was firing not out of but into it, so that my prison might be broken open like an egg. I chose the corner of my room that I thought would stand up best (the night I was driven here I glimpsed in the headlights a kind of *porte-cochère* of concrete, and I know where I am in relation to it); and standing against the wall I waited in a flood of hope that the mortar would draw return fire. I began to guess which of my guards were outside the door and what they would do if the building were hit and I made a run for it. Spiderman would shoot me because those would be his orders; but he would not like doing so, and he might therefore hesitate for a crucial few seconds if the others could not see him. Both Fuzzy and Sambo would probably panic and let me get away, and not be sorry to do so. Charley-boy would shoot to kill for pure pleasure. If one of them were badly wounded, could I run past him, or should I have to stop and help? (Not unless his need was desperate and he called to me, I thought. But it might be different in action.)

I stood in the corner while ten minutes went by after the last shots were fired; but no liberating destruction was loosed. The silence seeped back, and when I was quite sure that it would not be broken again I returned to my split and filthy table. But I did not finish the paragraph at once, because I was afraid that the quinine taste of disappointment would get into the text and turn it sour.

Not until the last few days did my captors tell me that they had been in touch with anyone about me, except their masters in Madras. I might have guessed that they had 'claimed' my kidnap, as boasting about criminal actions is the usual practice today, but for some reason I did not. Stupid situations tend to make us stupid, I think. I knew that they were in constant touch with Madras, and I took it for granted that whether they killed me or not would be at the whim of some thug there. I was prepared to leave it at that, because only thus could I be sure that bargaining with 'undesirable people' was not going on after all. But Kenyatta and the others supposed that I must want to be bargained for, and so could not understand why I was not begging them to get in touch with the British High Commissioner or any important person I could think of.

Mostly I pretended a complete lack of interest in anything going on around me; any detected spark of curiosity was likely to be taken as proof that I was a spy after all. I broke this rule once to ask Spiderman what the firing mentioned on the last page had been. He replied that there had been no firing, that he and the others had heard nothing. I saw that I should get no good by pressing him. But later in Colombo I learned that it had not been a contact with the security forces, it had been an exchange of fire between rival terrorist groups. The army had known roughly where I was at that time, because Tamil neighbours living near the house I was in had managed to get word out to them. Translated, the message as it reached army headquarters had included the phrase: 'Get these people off our backs'; and the senders had hoped that the need to rescue a foreigner would provoke action. And so it would have: the General who had told me he would not be able to help if it came to it was willing to have a go. But the British High Commission had asked him not to, lest the operation miscarry.

Once, Kenyatta volunteered that there was to be a debate in the House of Commons about me the next day. I knew that

that was nonsense, though it was possible that some MP might have been enlisted by my family to help in some way. I very much hoped not, because it would mean reports in the Press: free publicity for the terrorists, a thing which I was very anxious not to help them to. So we went on playing cat-and-mouse with each other, and I kept up my pretence of unconcern about my own fate: partly because I found that the easiest thing to do.

Meanwhile I asked Spiderman for another exercise-book, and went on writing about Greece. I had come further, in a few weeks' captivity, than just the distance from Mullaitivu to Jaffna, and I was ready now to write about the first time that I went to Crete, in 1953.

I had heard talk about the Samaria Gorge in the White Mountains, and it had worked on my imagination like yeast in a vat. So I scraped together every drachma I could, took five days off, and bought a ticket for Chania. The very people who had stirred me up then said that I could not go down the Gorge. Conditions in Crete were still too unsettled; the going was too bad for a woman alone; hardly any foreigners had ever been down it; law and order had never reached there yet ... After Chania I had better go to Rethymnon or somewhere reasonable. And who knows? Perhaps I would have, if it had not been for a letter from England.

That letter seemed so utterly and grotesquely unjust that I could not digest it at all. I knew that the writer could not know how unjust it was; and I also knew that the writer was half-demented at the time with worry and bewilderment. For all that, I felt as if there were a knife between my ribs, and the only way to pull it out and stop the bleeding was to take the same sort of course as had carried me to Zaltsa.

*

The head of the Samaria Gorge breaks away from the lip of a small plateau that lies like a handkerchief between the glittering limestone teeth of the White Mountains. The plateau is called the Omalos: a place of history. It was here that the *pallikaria* gathered in 1866 to launch the Cretan rebellion against the Turks — and a fitter place for that beginning would be hard to find. There is a tourist pavilion there now, and a motor road up to it. But when I went, the first few hundred yards of road were being cut by the men of the last village, in their own time, with state-supplied tools; and I saw a feat which I have never heard equalled anywhere. A man was wielding a sledge-hammer with his two arms, and at the same time controlling a pneumatic drill by leaning on it with his solar plexus. This is an example of the sort of exaggeration of normal life which besets and characterizes Cretan behaviour and makes the island so uniquely intoxicating.

The last 1,500 feet to the Omalos were by goat-track, and the plateau, furry with new grass and dotted here and there with flocks and one or two huts of branches, felt very good to walk on. The herdsmen there said I could not go down the gorge. First of all, the track was too difficult. Secondly, winter storms had carried it away in places, and no one had been down to make it good. Thirdly, a blood-feud was raging between themselves, the men of the Omalos, and the men of the village near the bottom of the gorge. They gave me milk and bread and tomatoes from a little patch of tilled ground beside one of the huts, and said that no one had been all the way up or down for three years. When they saw that I intended to go whatever was said, they gave up argument and instead loaded me with advice and details about the track. There was a place where an earlier rock-fall had carried it away completely for a hundred metres. One must make one's own way across, but be sure not to come out on a lower level than before, or there would be no hope of regaining the track; and so on. They took me on their donkey across the plateau, saying that to save a couple of miles' legwork would be worth while before I got to the end of my walk.

Once through the gorge, I planned to go on down the stream-bed the few miles to the sea. Here there was a village, Ayia Roumeli, and a frequented track, or even a boat, by which to get to Sphakia and a road-head. The herdsmen of the Omalos reckoned that Ayia Roumeli was seven hours' walk away.

They took me to the very lip of the gorge: a place where you stepped through some little rough trees, the ground rising slightly and a big shoulder of mountain straight in front of you; pushed aside the bushes; and found that the ground between you and that shoulder fell away down a thousand feet. They wished God with me, and one of them gave me his *katsouni*. These are shepherds' crooks, made as much for helping the user along in rough places as for catching sheep, and they are personal things, very rarely given away. I tried to refuse it, for each shepherd makes his own, choosing a branch off some tree on the mountainside, watching it grow till it is ready, cutting and trimming it, then soaking and shaping it for weeks before it is finished. So how would he manage until he had another one ready? But he would not touch it again, saying that I should need it; and I did.

At first the going was good, a small but clear path straggling and dividing as such paths always do but easy enough to follow, crawling not too steeply down the west-facing, left-hand side of the gorge. A strong and strange happiness took hold of me; I did not understand it, and did not try to. Presently I came to a stretch I could hardly have got across without the *katsouni*, and the bottom was a very long, inhospitable way down. I thought that if I were to slip, here, I should at the same time slip right off the earth. No one knew where I was, except the herdsmen on the Omalos, who knew nothing of me. One day, perhaps many weeks away because of the blood-feud, they would hear by grapevine if I had been through Ayia Roumeli; but they would not hear if I had not. They might guess that I had gone missing, but they would not know who to tell, so no telling would be done. The kites and the foxes would finish off the carcass and no one be a whit the wiser. This thought brought peace and a feeling of the rightness and proportion of things, and all seemed very good.

But now a much stranger sensation began to take hold of me. Each time I looked across at the crests on the other side of the gorge I had an impression of something very glorious up there. I could see that there was nothing: just rock and forest and more rock against the sky. But the picture that kept forming in my mind (not in the eyes) each time I looked, and staying each time a little longer, was of a chariot and horses of fire, carrying no Elijah, no Apollo even, but Jesus Christ himself.

I had been for years a total and happy pagan. I had nothing against Christianity, beyond what I took to be a slightly foolish attachment to superstition, and between sixteen and seventeen I had spent a year at a convent school which had left me with a real respect for the Catholic tradition. But the notion of a 'personal' god was simply incomprehensible to me, and I thought Christ no greater a man than several others. If I had been asked to make a list, I should probably have put Socrates at the top. So why was I making this, to me not significant, identification? It must be tiredness, I thought, or the heat, though I felt neither hot nor tired. Yet it became clearer and clearer to me that this sense (which was as strong and rational as the sense of well-being that warmth gives), of a great glory only just out of touching distance, was the source of my happiness: as the fire is the source of warmth.

There is a kind of inner recoil-and-release of mind which is surprise at another level. I began to see that perhaps I had been mistaken all these years, and that there may be times when man is less blind to the way in which his world is put together than other times. And when you feel the warmth of the fire it is not reasonable to say only that there can be no fire there. I saw that I must rethink a number of things I had supposed I was certain of. But I would think about them in the future: not now.

I came to that part of the track which the cliff-fall had swept away, and started across a face of loose rock and scree. I lost my footing once, and was saved by the *katsouni*, getting purchase with it on a torn root. Ahead there was a fathom or so of good, firm rock, and beyond that another reach of the same stuff as before. I stopped to study it, holding on to a little crooked thorn-tree that on the atoll of firm rock had survived the landslip. And there as I stood a steadying hand fell on my shoulder. I turned, but needlessly, for I knew there was no one there, nor could be. The invisible chariot was no longer on the skyline either, it was up and away; and here in its place, on this side of the gorge, touching my shoulder, was an immense and infallible reassurance. Nothing will happen that shouldn't happen. If you fall, it doesn't matter; if you get across, it doesn't matter either: be grateful and go on. There is nothing to fear, either way.

I did not see it for many years, but the thought underlying this was: 'Only guilt or freedom from it matters, and there is no guilt in falling. Therefore discount it.' But at the same time I had just been taught something which I had never had an inkling of before. I had been made to know the touch of God, and I should never again be able in honesty to doubt His existence. Nor have I; and the same reassurance has come to me again in other ways in my present predicament.

For the time being, however, I was half-blinded, and deliberately did not think about what had happened. I found the path again, and presently saw goat-droppings on it. But there was no sound, no near or distant tonk of a bell nor the give-away rustle of a falling stone under narrow hooves. Before long the track debouched on to a broad, green mountain-lawn filling a bay of flat ground where the wall of the gorge fell back a little. Huge native cypresses grew here, dark-shaded and silvery-barked. The grass was thick with wild larkspur, and set

172

back against the rock-face among the trees was a very small, very neglected chapel. I went in. Everything was dark, the floor and the icons blackened with smoke and candle-grease, both old, and there were no candles there now to be lighted. The iconostasis was in place, but so battered and blackened that its saints were unrecognizable except for one, which showed that the church was dedicated to St Nicholas. I left a few drachmae (what I thought I could afford, which was not much) in a box beside the candle-sconce; not that it seemed likely that a priest would soon arrive to tidy up and would collect them. Then I went on down until I came to the village.

It was a huddle of huts at a point where a side-stream joins the main gorge; they stood at a bridge, on a low rock bluff overlooking the track, so no one was likely to get past unobserved. I was seen at once; and even though I had come down from the territory of the enemy up at the Omalos (there was nowhere else I could have come from, unless an eagle had dropped me) still hospitality prevailed, and every woman in the village — probably at least a dozen — pressed me to stay in her house. But it was very strong on me that, for whatever reason, I was neither fit nor ready for human company. So I used the only excuse which could ever serve. I said that I had promised to go on down to Ayia Roumeli, that I was expected there. It sounded hopelessly unlikely. By whom? I fell back on language difficulty. I thought that I was telling a lie: I had no inkling yet of who was waiting for me.

At last, after making me eat some very terrible food, they let me go. If the men had been there I should not have got away with it, but they were all up the mountain. The women were mystified about this, for the men must all have been round about St Nicholas when I passed through. I had actually stopped there, and been into the church? Even if the men had been asleep in one of the caves (since it had been in the mid-afternoon) the dogs could not have failed to hear me, and would have wakened the dead. I could see that they were deeply puzzled. For two pins I think they might have believed in an eagle.

I went on downwards, and the light turned slowly to apricot and the sky to melon-red. I began to look for a place where I could get off the track and sleep for the night, having no more wish to spend it in Ayia Roumeli than in the last village. The track and the stream-bed were now very close together, the one sometimes dipping down into the other. I was going through a little grove of trees at a place where the gorge widened out, when I heard shouts behind me, then the pounding of hooves on the stones, clattering like a cannonade and echoing back off the rocks. A huge, pure-white mule came round a bend of the track at a hand-gallop, rope harness flying. I stood in its path with my arms spread out, and it swerved just before I had to; then, once its head was turned uphill and toward the rock-face, it slowed and came to a jolting stop. I went to it and took the head-rope, and it stood quietly until a man in high boots came into sight, stopped running, reached us, and took the rope from me. He said that as he was starting to load the mule it had jerked free, shaken off the saddle, and gone as if the devil were behind it. Never in its life had it done so before. And now look at it, as quiet as a lamb.

But, he went on, the affair was lucky too. It had been wrong of the women to let me go, because it would be dark soon and much too dangerous for me to be in the gorge alone. But he was himself going down to Ayia Roumeli; he must go back now to reload the mule, but he would overtake me and see me safely through. And he set off briskly up the track again, with the beast following docilely behind him.

I was now in a quandary; but I saw that this incident had really been lucky for me, though not in the way he meant. For now that I knew he was coming down behind me, I could stay out of sight until he had gone past. I was filled with an overwhelming desire to be alone. I found a comfortable cranny and after fifteen minutes or so saw the man and his mule pass below me. He was singing now, and once or twice broke off to call out loudly. I felt guilty, but I kept quiet.

When I could no longer hear the clink of the stones under

the mule's hooves I moved on again. I was tired by this time, and slipped and fell into the water several times, but did myself no damage. The light was greying and ebbing: it would not last another half-hour. I thought I had better find a place for myself before it had gone altogether.

Round the next turn the cliffs opened out again; a few feet above the stream-bed there was a smooth, grassy space, and behind that, sloping up the cliff, a narrow wood of silver firs. In the middle of the grass stood a church even smaller than St Nicholas': perhaps ten or twelve feet long, with two planks that had once been a door leaning up loose against the jamb.

Someone had been logging down here, a season or more ago: there were dry grey chips lying in profusion. I piled a few together, with thyme for tinder, and lit a small fire to dry myself by. While it was taking hold I went to the church. I moved the planks to one side, looked in — and stopped dead in my tracks, with that tingling from head to heels that terror or great excitement can bring. There was no iconostasis, I was looking directly into the apse of the church, and at a round-topped unglazed window. This window blazed with light, and through it, leaning half on the sill, half on his crook, a shepherd looked in. He was smiling, almost laughing. His expression, in the second in which I saw it, said: 'You thought you'd get away from me, didn't you? But you see you can't.' His eyes were gentle, yet openly mocking, brimming with an elemental joy. I do not know whether I looked away, or whether mind took hold again over something that had momentarily displaced it. For mind was hammering three messages to me: the sun set half an hour ago; you are looking east; and you are 3,000 feet down in a gorge. Then my eyes resumed their habit, and I saw that there was no window (mind knew too that there could not be). But on the crumbled ruin of the iconostasis was one very magnificent icon of the Virgin and Child, with a pure gold background. Some last ray of light from the doorway behind me must have caught the gold and

175

deluded me.* I stepped outside again, knowing in my bones that this, which my mind had just offered me, was not in truth what I had seen: and that what I had seen was irreversible. Something had happened which had radically altered my relation with the world round me. But just what it was, I was still not ready to think out. It was nearly six months, in fact, before I came to terms with it, and that under the pressure of great sorrow.

In the last of the dusk I gathered silver-fir branches and thyme-brush for bedding, for it was cold now and I had only a jersey for warmth. I dried myself at the fire, and ate the bread and olives that I had with me, and drank from the stream. Then I put one of the door-planks down on the earth floor of the church, and the greenery on top of it; for the Orthodox tradition is that a traveller without a night's shelter may sleep in a church without the least impiety, and a woman especially is right to do so. I trod out the last of the fire: the sparks fled and were lost among swarms of great gold stars crowding the sky. I went inside and lay down and pulled the thyme over me and slept.

I woke in the morning to the scrape of a boot on stone. I sat up and looked round. There was bright sunlight outside, and in the doorway, looking down at me astonished, stood a shepherd. I said 'Good morning' for I could think of nothing else to say. He wished me the same; and then, unable to wait through all the formalities: 'Why . . .?' I said that I had been tired the night before: I could go no further. His face cleared, for that was understandable. He said that they had waited for me at Ayia Roumeli. The man with the mule did not know how he had come to miss me. I asked what this place was called, and he said 'Samaria'. It means 'mule-saddles', but I did not know that at the time: I could only connect it with the familiar Samaria. He asked my name and I gave it: my Christian name, for that is the one that counts in the Greek countryside. Surnames are new-found things, often no more than a century or two old, and good only for purposes of officialdom. The

* Later I learned that no such icon had ever been there.

176

honourable name is the one God knows you by. I asked him, as politeness requires, for his. 'Christos,' he answered.

I went down to the stream and washed in it; and we walked away up the gorge together.

What new things do we hope to find when we travel? There is no end to them, and no guessing what kind they may be. There are those who say that the real (not just the geographical and material) discoveries can all be made in one place as well as in another: that you can reach the stars while you stay at home. That is true for the good and the wise, but not for the bad and foolish. Blessed are the meek, for they shall inherit the earth. Those of us who are not meek must go to look for our inheritance elsewhere, and may find it in empty places or among strangers, or, if we are blessed beyond expectation, in the human heart. But we are exiles. Nothing that we find here will ever belong to us, nor we to it.

And was it this kind of travelling, this seeking of inheritance, that has brought me here at last, to sit behind bars like an animal in a cage? Yes. Do I repent it? I repent the pain brought to those three whom I love with my heart and soul. But for myself, no. I am not being beaten or tortured, and whatever happens to me I shall have brought on myself, so there is nothing to complain about. However, I have prayed as best I can, though I still do not know how to pray, and tried my best to trust. I have begun to doubt that they will kill me, after all. In any case I accepted the idea of that earlier on. I have had such very good things in life that I should be ashamed to beg or cling in hopes of still more. One of the things I have come to see while killing time here is how pitifully few good things most of mankind enjoy: I do not mean materially, not because physical circumstances are against them, but because they have asked for things other than joy. (So have I: but my good angel has known better.)

I lack the patience to be a prisoner, even for the short time, four weeks, which is all I have yet had of it. Writing this has helped me to keep myself in hand, and I am correspondingly grateful to my gaolers for giving me paper. They are the detritus of a spurious revolutionary movement. They have little or no understanding of what is at stake, and probably some of them are not bad in themselves. I doubt that they would burn a man alive, for instance. Yet they know that their leaders do this, and still they follow them. They have fallen in with the wrong lot, and cannot get out because they do not know how to think for themselves.

These people are only a random handful of the debris that of late years has been sucked up and thrown into our eyes on Drazha Mihailovic's 'gale of the world'. I hope to write later about that gale, if I survive it myself: about what vacuum set it blowing; whether and when it may be laid. Meantime, if this book gets out of the vortex with me, and if anyone should read it through to here, let me propose a final, revised word on real travelling. Those of us who do it are only trying to find the road back to Paradise.

I reached the end of what I have written here about Greece before I could guess at all what the end of my imprisonment would be. But the story I have just recounted, which took place in Crete, was reflected in Jaffna.

A morning came when I reached a very low ebb. I had begun to see that my captors had nothing to gain by letting me go. They surely knew by now that they were not going to extract a ransom or some concession from the government in exchange for me; nor were they going to get the 'good propaganda' they had named to me as their price. And by now they had kept me long enough to have lost any credit they might have claimed for releasing me as an act of clemency. On top of this I thought (wrongly) that the mechanics of a release were difficult for them and possibly dangerous. Nor could they simply turn me loose in Jaffna, lest one of the other groups should take over where they left off; I had already seen how unacceptable that notion is to terrorists. I thought that at the next interrogation I would put it to them that they were getting no good out of holding me: I was an unnecessary expense and liability, might well be the cause of attacks by the security forces, and must be earning them a bad press abroad. I would suggest that, to avoid the risk to themselves of a proper handover, they should take me back to wherever they had left my car, put me into it, and let me take my chance of finding my own way out.

Kenyatta had that day broken off an interrogation, saying he would be back in the morning. I waited eagerly for his arrival (a change in itself), but three days later there was still no sign of him nor of any of the 'seniors'. Even Spiderman seemed to be off duty. It grew upon me more and more strongly that there was no real reason why they should ever let me go. To do anything would be more trouble for them than to do nothing. I might therefore be facing a sentence not of a few days or weeks but of years.

It is very much more difficult to confront an indeterminate future of that kind than to look down a gun barrel. Instead I looked up from the table: and found that I was not alone. It would have been easy to write 'saw', but I saw nothing. What was before me was stronger than sight. It was the presence of Our Lady: not visible, not tangible, but inside the four walls that stood round me and more real than they. I had often been advised to pray to her when life looked black, but I had never had the least idea how to do so or what she might be. Now she was a few feet away from me, not intruding, not asking that I know her or accept her help, but saying simply: 'I am here: use me or not, as you like.' She did not say: 'I will make things right for you,' or 'I will not let that happen.' Nor was there any trace of a bargain: 'Trust me,' (or 'believe in me'), 'and I will help you.' Only: 'I am with you, through the valley

179

of the shadow or anywhere else, from this moment on. But I shall never force myself on you. You need never know that I am here unless you want to; and unless you want to, you need never again be alone.'

Nor have I been, since then, nor ever shall be.


Events may be given impetus from outside or generate their own, but either way they flag when it fails. Some time in the fourth week of prison I became aware that the impetus bearing my captors towards murder was no longer there.

I was, however, extraordinarily slow and stupid about interpreting small events. One afternoon Spiderman and Charley-boy came into my room with a camera and took five or six photographs of me, making me first sit then stand close against the wall, and using a flashlight. They kept exhorting me to smile while they did this. I was in fact unreasonably concerned about what was the right expression, and about maintaining it. They said the photographs were wanted in Madras, and I thought that any hint of a smile on my face would be produced by EROS as evidence of what a nice lot they were and how well I was getting on with them. At the same time, to look too down in the mouth might convey that they were getting the better of me, and at all costs I was not going to give them that fillip. I settled upon what I hoped was a suitably boot-faced look.

I thought that they must want these photographs either for self-promotion in the Madrassi Press or for comparison with a photograph file there, in some further effort to find out who or what I was. Or they might want them as proof that they had got me, for purposes of negotiation with my own or the Sri Lankan government. As I did not want to be negotiated for (more accurately, I wanted it passionately, but was set fast against it), and as I was confident that I had insured safely against it, I was not interested in that line of thought. But somehow it never struck me that the photographs might be a preliminary to release.

180

A few days later they came and took a second set. Fuzzy was allowed to work the camera this time so I thought it unlikely that anything would come out; he seemed hardly to know which way up to hold it. This time it passed through my mind that they might be considering letting me go and wanted to make sure they could recognize me if I ever turned up again. But the idea did not hold me. I wanted no truck with false hopes.

Dusk each evening brought the mosquitoes out. Whether they spent the days sleeping on the ceiling or infiltrated through the ventilator at the top of the wall I never learned, for the frosted glass kept the light dim; but I thought that they must lead strange lives. I was grateful to them in one way, because their arrival brought out a pair of geckos. These too must have slept during the day in a crack between wall and ceiling, but once awake they were lively little companions, prowling and stalking and snapping up insects, with their enormous heads holding such little brains and their mouths set in innocent-looking saurian smiles. I watched while one of them sat seemingly in a long trance, as they so often do, while the other, at right angles to it, stalked its next mouthful. But when the victorious rush came it was not on to a mosquito, it was to make a great snap at the belly of the other gecko. The target was too big: the gaping jaws could not close, no damage was done, and a moment or two later the war against the mosquitoes went on as usual. They were like the warring liberationists: believing themselves capable of any grandiose feat, and murderous from lack of mind.

More days went by during which I saw no one. Then late one night I was roused from bed by Lobster-Eyes, who ordered me to take pen and exercise-book and dictated a great quantity of inept Tamil propaganda. He left well after midnight, saying he would be back at breakfast time. I never saw him again. Nor did anyone else come for two days, then Spiderman reappeared and ordered me to write every detail of my journey from Anuradhapura to Mullaitivu and from Mullaitivu to

181

Jaffna. I wrote at great length and in suffocating detail without a word about anything that they could possibly want to know. They made me do it again in a large, round, clear hand. Even then Spiderman got me to read it aloud to him, following with a finger along the lines to verify that the words I was saying were the same as I had written.

He took this away and brought it back the next day, saying I must add to it a statement of my personal view of how I had been treated, and my 'personal request' to the organization in Madras — presumably for my release, though that was not said.

I took my time over this, putting together a paragraph which I reckoned could not be made to read as condoning their actions or exonerating them, however they might pick phrases out of context. But I did write that, once the first week of violence and threats was over, the small fry who had been my keepers had not ill-treated me or behaved badly towards me. It seemed only just to say that. And I finished not with a request but a flat though polite statement that my release was both necessary and long overdue.

When I was told that this too must be written in large round-hand, I said that EROS must be a pretty inferior organization if it could not rustle up a typewriter.

'But,' said Spiderman, 'none of us can type.'

I said, 'Well, I can.' He looked suitably checkmated, and next morning appeared with a portable Olivetti, fairly heavily damaged but quite usable, and a supply of paper and carbons. The day that followed was the most comfortable I had yet spent, because I insisted that if I was to work as a typist for them I must have the door open for fresh air. I do not think they would have given in to this as an argument for itself, but they all wanted to watch the typing and were not themselves willing to put up with the stifling heat of an airless room. So the door was left open on to the hallway, which itself had french windows on to a little fenced garden, and the first air for three weeks blew through while I sat typing twaddle (they

182

wanted the whole preceding screed typed as well, now) and two of them at a time stood outside on sentry-go while the other two stood behind me and watched as if I were performing the three-card trick at a fair.

When the job was done they locked me up again and carried the typewriter away. But that night on my way to the washroom I saw it on a table in the hall. Charley-boy was sitting in front of it with a look of bliss on his face, prodding with different fingers at keys and other parts of it while Fuzzy fairly danced round him, making stabbing gestures of his own towards it. Not only might a pair of those grey langurs from Nilaveli have behaved much the same around a machine: no small thing I think could have shown more vividly what those people are like, who with the aid of weapons and explosives and pompous speeches busy themselves making the world dance to their tune.

So far as I know no use was ever made of that typed report. (After all, I had designed it to be useless.)


A day or two later Kenyatta arrived to say that I must be ready to move in about twenty minutes. It could hardly have taken me two minutes to be ready, but I was used to notifications that this or that was about to happen, followed by nothing whatsoever. This time I stood-to for about three hours, and was resigning myself to the usual pattern when the door crashed open, re-admitting Kenyatta. He personally checked that I left nothing behind; then I was marched out and into a waiting Japanese jeep. He, Spiderman, and three others all got in too (so we were a fairly tight load) and we were away.

A drive of twenty minutes or half an hour followed, through outskirts of the town, finishing up outside a luxurious-looking villa well fenced and surrounded by flowering shrubs and armed men. Kenyatta went into it. I got out of the jeep; I was cramped and stiff and glad of the stretch, but after a moment's indecision I was ordered back in. A long wait ensued; then

Kenyatta returned, Charley-boy got out, someone else got in, and we were off again.

I had had two strong impressions from this place: that it belonged to someone senior in the organization, and that there had been either a muddle or a sudden change of plans. Orders had been countermanded and no one knew what to do next. However we were quickly overtaken by an armed motorcyclist who signalled to our driver to follow him, and thus guided we slithered and bumped away over sandy tracks for another quarter of an hour.

Much later, when I was free again, I learned that there had indeed been an offer to release me at this time. EROS in Madras had agreed that I be handed over to a representative of the Red Cross; a member from London had flown out to Colombo, and she and a member of the British High Commission had flown to Jaffna to fetch me. But the agreement had not been honoured. They had waited in Jaffna for two days and then had to return to Colombo empty-handed.

Looking back, I can guess that EROS in Madras had got tired of the operation, and taken it for granted that when they asked for a 'personal request' from me they would get one, in a form which they could use to show themselves in a good light. What I had sent them was of no use, so they scrubbed the plan, but most likely it was only when we got to the villa that Kenyatta heard of the change.

Late that night we stopped at a big sprawling bungalow on the edge of a village, in the angle between two roads. Here there were a number of armed men, inside and out, and I was given a chair amongst them in the hall and told to wait. Everyone seemed confused; Spiderman and his team disappeared and I could hear furniture being lugged about. A very tall, very thin, very old lady came and sat beside me, and made me welcome in halting English which had once been fluent. It dawned on me that this was her house, and that she was living 'under occupation' as the phrase used to be. To be keeping her up at this hour made me feel guilty and bad-mannered, though there was nothing I could do about it. She told me that she was a Roman Catholic, and this lifted my spirits in two ways: for itself, and because it made me think that the idea of releasing me must after all be in the air. Almost all they knew about me was that I am a Catholic, so this would be a propaganda move. If and when they did release me, selected journalists would be drafted in to report as much, and to say how considerately I had been provided for.

The window in the room now allotted to me had been nailed up and the glass behind the bars smeared with paint, but the room had no door, only a curtain. This did not mean any greater chance of escape, because of the larger number of armed men now outside it at all times (strangers, too, who would probably have less compunction about killing me than those who had known me willy-nilly for a month), and because of the old lady and her brother, who would no doubt have to pay, perhaps with their lives, for any misdemeanour of mine. But the curtain admitted air; not a lot, it is true, and a bit smelly because the washroom (marginally better than the last one) was alongside. Still, any air is better than none. I could go in and out of the washroom when I liked; the guards could always see me coming and going but I did not have to bang for them and be taken there. This felt like a real luxury; and to make it more so Spiderman brought me a pair of plastic flip-flops with which to go in and out of it. Civilization was being allowed to seep back. The greatest luxury of all was an electric ceiling-fan, which the old lady kindly urged me to use when I wanted to. I thought she had not much to live on, and I was fairly sure that the terrorists were not going to pay her electricity bill, so I did not use it much; but when the afternoon heat was beating full on the shut window and the room felt like the inside of a boiler it was a godsend to get a quarter of an hour of whirling coolness.

Nevertheless the days began to drag very heavily. Kenyatta

looked in and told me to write two letters. One was to be to the British High Commissioner in Colombo, and was to beg him to arrange, as the price of my release, for a member of the International Red Cross to come to Jaffna and take delivery of me. I had no intention of letting myself be used as a lever to raise these people to the status of internationally recognized belligerents. I had already been asked rhetorically, many times, why the Sri Lankan government would not have the International Red Cross here to mediate between the government and the terrorists; each time I had said that the Tamil problem here was not one which the ICRC could handle, under the terms of its charter. The Sri Lankan or British Red Cross Societies could and would help victims, if the terrorists would let them.

Sticking to this line therefore, I now wrote to the High Commissioner that I was under orders to make such a request to him, and that I knew that under ICRC rules it could not be complied with. I did, however, ask him to telephone to Tony on my behalf.

It was to Tony that Kenyatta told me to write the second letter. Perhaps he still hoped for some indiscretion which he could twist into evidence of guilt. I kept to the same subjects as before.

I asked how these two letters were to go, for this was the first time I had been given any hint that EROS were in touch with the High Commissioner or anyone else in Colombo. Kenyatta said someone on a motor-bicycle would take them, and deliver one to the High Commission and the other to the main post office. I thought about this and came to the conclusion that though it could easily be done he was almost certainly lying. Whether he was or not, I learned later that neither letter was ever sent.


The last week in that house stays in my mind as the worst. There were no books now; I had finished a tidy draft of the

Greek part of this one; I started to write on another subject, but needed references without which it was hard to bring it along in the way I wanted. Then I ran out of paper and no more seemed available; at any rate, no more was supplied. Spiderman found and brought me two copies of *Life* magazine, both over two years old so scarcely thrilling. But to fill in the time I read every syllable of them and the solider parts several times over. At the foot of one page I found one of those tear-off coupons which the reader is invited to complete with his name and address and send off, in order to be put on some mailing list. It had been filled in, in pencil, with the name Rosalyn Thomas, and the first part of an American-sounding address.

I sat for a long time wondering about it. Kenyatta and Spiderman had both reminded me that Tamils had kidnapped a woman more than a year before and that nothing had been heard of her since. And since we had come to this house they had told me that an American couple, kidnapped and held for a week more recently, had been kept here. I had reason to think that the second story was true, and I had understood why they had told me the first: to remind me that I might have years of oblivion ahead. I had learned by now to believe little or nothing that they said. But now I sat and wondered whether this half-completed coupon was someone's desperate hope of some day getting word out to the real world: a clutch at a chance not much better than that of a bottle thrown into the sea. When I got out I tried to verify whether any missing person was recorded as Rosalyn Thomas, and was hugely relieved to hear that none was known of. After all, then, the name was only of some would-be shopper whose impulse had died. I was never given the chance to ask the old lady about it. But the magazine might have reached that house at third, fourth, fifth hand; off a ship or an aeroplane; brought down by one of the terrorists from Madras; who knows now?

*

My room here contained an easy chair so life should have been more comfortable. But my spine was now so painful that I could not sit there for more than about five minutes unless I put the rigid bolster from the bed (there was one here too) upright in the chair like a Victorian back-board. So I moved about restlessly from easy chair to bed to hard chair and round again. There were no geckos here for company but very many mosquitoes, whose dances up and down the whitewashed glass had an airy grace which I liked to watch. In the evenings they were like wolves, and I was correspondingly thankful to Spiderman for bringing me coils of fumigant. He found the smell of these unbearable himself, but it seemed was under orders not to allow me to get malaria; they had established that I had not had the usual course of pills against it.

My greatest pleasure came from watching the little cat that lived in the house: the narrowest, thinnest, most sinuous and silent of black cats, with huge sea-green eyes and ears like sails. Its fur was not in the least lustrous; it was like the blackness of a sleepless night. This little creature would now and then slide in past the door-curtain and make a thorough search of the room wall by wall, standing on its hind legs and stretching up as far as its paws could reach, and catching and eating mosquitoes whenever they came too near. Then it would climb all the furniture, with the same thoroughness and a kind of quiet desperation that made it too seem like a prisoner. Doing physically what I was doing in mind, it seemed like a true companion.

The bars on the window were set horizontally, four inches apart. One day the cat jumped for the sill, clung on, and climbed straight up the bars as if they were a ladder, almost to the top; then it looked down, suddenly lost hold, and fell, hitting the table and knocking my water-glass to the floor with a tremendous crash but without hurting itself. Two of the guards came running, guns in hand, to see what was happening, then stood looking foolishly round. But the little cat slipped out past them like an eddy of smoke.

*

Kenyatta came in one afternoon with a sheet of newsprint which he told me to read. It carried one of the photographs of me which had been taken in the other house, and a text purporting to be a record of an interrogation of me by someone unnamed. It was mostly fiction, apart from information gathered from my passport. Most of the misstatements did not matter — and where my captors were ignorant I saw no particular purpose in enlightening them; but I complained about some points and Kenyatta said he would have them put right. I asked where this stuff was to appear, and he said, in a Madras daily. The headline to the piece was THE WOMAN IS A DIRTY SPY, which was less than encouraging.

Yet at this time my gaolers' manner towards me was growing not sterner but less so. I therefore thought that, though I had better be ready to make a run for it at any time, I need not act for the moment. The air was charged with change of one kind or another, and I found it increasingly hard to keep my mind on anything.

Next day Kenyatta was back, with a Jaffna paper called, I think, *Weekend*. It contained the piece he had shown me before, without the corrections he had promised. When I pointed this out he only shrugged and said something like 'Never mind'. Then he said: 'I think we shall hand you over tomorrow morning.' I said: 'Who to?' He looked surprised and said: 'To your friends.' Then he shot me an inquisitor's glance, as if he thought there might be something to be extracted from me even yet. (Or perhaps he just did not believe that I was too stupid to have understood what had been going on.) I said: 'Does anybody know where I am?'

'No.'

'Then how will you hand me over?'

'We shall see.'

Next morning nothing happened. I had not really expected that anything would; none the less, I dare say it was the longest morning I have spent in my life.

About two in the afternoon there was a great clattering

through the hall and four young men with Kalashnikovs filed into the room. I said, 'Good afternoon,' and one of them mumbled a reply. They sat down in a row on the bed and stared at me. After a time one, who had a little English, began asking questions of the usual interrogation type, in an impertinent, would-be worldly manner which gave away that he did not know what he was asking them for. I thought I had had enough of this and simply stopped answering, and they all sat there staring and giggling and twisting their rifles about between their knees. If these are the People's Representatives, I thought, who are going to run this island when it is unified under Marxism, then goodbye to 2,500 years of hard-won civilization, and God help the People.

Spiderman had stood behind them as they filed in, gazing at them, I had thought, with unreserved admiration; but even he seemed disillusioned with their performance, and when they suddenly got up and left, all together and apparently reasonlessly like starlings off a tree, he looked thoroughly relieved.

The afternoon dragged on. Fuzzy came in and seemed very anxious to say something. He had no word of English, but I grasped from his gestures that he wanted me to give him my watch. This seemed to confirm that I was to be let go, or at least that Fuzzy thought so. I would have given it to him if I had been sure, but I could not face the prospect of remaining a prisoner, and only God could know for how long, without it. Besides, I knew that to ask for it was a grave infringement of Mao's rules and could get Fuzzy into serious trouble. He showed clearly that he knew he was doing wrong, but he could not resist the temptation. All of them had watches except him.

And now here is another example of how difficult it is to handle this question of relationships between prisoners and gaolers if you allow the smallest step out of line. Writing this just now, I have found, felt like a disloyalty towards Fuzzy, since it is slightly to his discredit, and he was never other than good to me within the limitations of his job and his mind. Yet he was a potential murderer and henchman of murderers. It would be a misplaced loyalty in me to present him as other than he was; and misplaced loyalties can do immeasurable damage, most especially to real and rightly placed ones.

Some time after Fuzzy had gone Kenyatta reappeared and said curtly: 'Come.' I said, 'Should I take my things?' pointing to my towel.

'Yes, take them.'

Probably another gaol, then. I put them back into their plastic bag, and while I was doing so the old lady came in, with Spiderman behind her looking apologetically at Kenyatta because he had not been able to keep her away. I failed to understand what she was saying at first. She was telling me that Lent had started and that she had brought the Holy Chrism from church that morning so that she could anoint me with it; and to the wonder of Kenyatta and Spiderman she did so while they watched. Then for good measure she turned and, before he could stop her, anointed Spiderman too. With the sign of the Cross in oil and ashes on his forehead, he stood there half ashamed and half trying to look superior to such things, but at bottom unable at this moment to be rude to her in front of me. It was Kenyatta who cut things short.

Outside the gate a Volkswagen Beetle was waiting. I was put into it with Spiderman, Sambo and Kenyatta and we drove off. Ahead of us was a motor-cycle carrying an armed man behind the driver, behind us a Japanese school-type bus filled with armed men, and behind that another armed motor-cycle pair. Whoever all this was meant to impress it drew no signs of enthusiasm for the 'liberators' as we made our way through crowded streets with horns blaring and engines roaring. This must have been how the Nazis moved about German cities, I thought, in the early days when they were setting up their power; or the servants of any tyranny beginning to establish its grip on a helpless population.

We pulled up at last in front of a long, low building set back from the road in a compound with a high wire fence, a gate, and a man in control of it. There were a few women in the compound; more came to join them and then more until they were a small crowd, quite silent, staring at us — or rather, at me. Were they friendly? Hostile? Waiting to see what would happen? Just killing time? I could not tell.

Kenyatta got out and disappeared into a house across the road. I asked Spiderman what we were here for. 'We are waiting for someone,' he said. It was very hot in the full sun. He too got out, and went to stand under a tree some yards away. The motor-cycle escort drove off but the bus and its load remained. (I had already noted its number; the motor-cycles had had no plates.) Half an hour ticked by; forty minutes. It became clear to me that this was simply their routine administrative muddle, on the way to another place of imprisonment. Kenyatta came back to the car and said: 'We are going now.'

'Where to?'

He looked shifty — that is, more so than ordinarily. 'To another place.'

I felt as if I had been dropped down a well, although I had expected nothing else. Sambo said something to him and got out and walked away from the car. Kenyatta said to me: 'In a minute.' We waited. Then Spiderman called from a little distance behind us, and there was a short interchange. Someone else was calling to Spiderman from round the corner. Abruptly and roughly, as if things had suddenly turned sour, Kenyatta said to me, 'Get out,' and when I was standing on the pavement, 'Go forward: they are there.' People were swarming round us; I saw an ambulance drawn up to the kerb, and walking towards me, not ten paces from me, a bearded stranger, unmistakably English, and a young woman in the uniform of the British Red Cross. As the distance shortened between us I would not let myself run, but I thought that we should never reach each other. Then we were shaking

192

hands, and the sun still shining, and the pavement firm under our feet.

Never trust anyone who kills and imprisons people while saying he is winning them their freedom. Never believe that the man is a victim who takes his neighbour's house by force and says it is self-defence. Never take a bully at his own valuation as a hero.

When it comes to the finer detail of the problem (and after all, kidnapping may be anyone's problem: we are all potential victims today) I would offer suggestions on two points.

Firstly, don't over-estimate the intelligence of your captors. Terrorism is a moron's occupation: if the killers and bombers had good minds they would be doing better things. Almost every major mistake I made came from supposing that my interrogators had put two and two together and made four. Over and over again it came out that they had not even tried to, let alone succeeded.

And it is fatally easy to suppose that they know much more than they do. They say so all the time, and you slip into accepting the idea. Because in physical terms they have complete power over you, you tend (or I tended) to exaggerate their importance. It is necessary to remember all the time that they are driven by one engine only: the desire to dominate. Intelligent men may succumb to this as well as stupid ones, but they find more intelligent methods than terrorism. And some of these involve making use of terrorists, of their blind vanity and contempt for others. I cannot generalize about the minds of the puppeteers. But it is not they whom you and I are likely to come face to face with, it is only their manikins, who jerk and dangle at the strings' ends, and lob a bomb into a crowd of strangers in the belief that they are reshaping society. Let us not help to build up their illusions about themselves. The greatest of these is that they are fighters in a noble cause, to whom anything is therefore allowed. They see bullying as heroism, and in their eyes it is not they who are terrorists but those who stand against them. They see the murders that they or their superiors commit as the fault of the government which refuses to give them their way; and if they do not torture their prisoners, that proves to them that they are kind and generous.

At all costs I want to say, never accept the hand of friendship from such people. Do not be deluded by any cant about compassion; it is neither godlike nor humanly right to go along with indiscriminate murder, and that is what you are doing if you make friends with hostage-takers.

Are you tempted to say: Yes, but this man who actually stands talking to me in my cell: he is a human being too, he has not shot me so far, and I don't know if he has shot anyone else. Have I not a duty of compassion towards him? And is there not a chance that he might change his approach to life if I let him see I understand that he too has a point of view? Believe me, he is very much likelier to shoot the next victim he gets in your stead, if you have encouraged him to think that his point of view has attracted your sympathy.

Or you might think: Have I not the right to feign sympathy, whatever my real views, when my life and liberty are at risk? Yes. But are they worth buying at that price?

During one of many interrogations (I have purposely not told you where or when) one man was called away briefly and I was left alone with the other. He went on as before for a moment; then I heard him say without the smallest change in inflection or tempo: 'If you get out alive tell the government the Tamil people do not want this Movement. They are not Marxist, they are good people, very religious, they don't want anything to do with Marxism. If you get out alive, say that. What do you know about . . .' Without a ripple to reveal the change of tack he went on with the interrogation.

Could that message have been given to me if I had been

feigning sympathy for the terrorists' views? And did the Tamil people he spoke for not need to have it given? I submit that if men cannot speak truthfully to each other life is simply not worth having: a sorry sham, no more than a breeding-ground for child-molesters and murderers. And if it sometimes looks like that now, the more reason for making a stand. Good luck to you: it is never too late.

## Author's Note

As my imprisonment lasted only weeks, not months or years, I feel there may be something unjustifiably boastful about the title of this book. I did not intend to boast; and after all, cages are of many kinds.